Thespians

Greece the Musical (Not That One)

Jonathan Sayer and Ed Zanders

methuen | drama
LONDON • NEW YORK • OXFORD • NEW DELHI • SYDNEY

METHUEN DRAMA
Bloomsbury Publishing Plc, 50 Bedford Square, London, WC1B 3DP, UK
Bloomsbury Publishing Inc, 1359 Broadway, New York, NY 10018, USA
Bloomsbury Publishing Ireland, 29 Earlsfort Terrace, Dublin 2, D02 AY28, Ireland

BLOOMSBURY, METHUEN DRAMA and the Methuen Drama logo are trademarks of Bloomsbury Publishing Plc.

First published in 2026 by Methuen Drama

Cover design: Steph Pyne

A catalogue record for this book is available from the British Library.

A catalog record for this book is available from the Library of Congress.

ISBN: PB: 978-1-3506-5240-8
ePDF: 978-1-3506-5242-2
eBook: 978-1-3506-5241-5

Series: Modern Plays

Typeset by Mark Heslington Ltd, Scarborough, North Yorkshire

For product safety related questions contact productsafety@bloomsbury.com.

To find out more about our authors and books visit www.bloomsbury.com and sign up for our newsletters.

HOME Manchester, Mercury Theatre Colchester & JPT Productions originally commissioned and presented the world premiere of the Mischief production *Thespians* in Colchester at the Mercury Theatre on 9 May 2026, followed by a UK tour with the following cast and creative team:

Rhapsodes	**Allie Dart**
Poly	**Claire-Marie Hall**
Thespis	**James Spence**
Atlas	**Luke Latchman**
Adonis	**Marc Pickering**
Bard	**Matt Cavendish**
Melampus	**Mia Jerome**
The Tyrant	**Rhys Taylor**
A Greek Chorus Line/ Understudies	**Ashley Tucker, Curtis Patrick, Josh Patel-Foster**

Book & Lyrics	Jonathan Sayer
Music & Lyrics	Ed Zanders
Directed by	Robyn Grant
Designed by	Jasmine Swan
Choreography	Melody Sinclair
Lighting Design	David Howe
Sound Design	Nick Lodge
Musical Director	Ben Smith
Associate Director	Joe Allen
Executive Producer	Henry Lewis

Presented by arrangement with Mischief Worldwide Ltd.

MISCHIEF creates award-winning comedy for stage, screen and beyond, with shows continuously playing in the West End for over a decade. Now a global sensation, they are currently bringing joy and laughter to audiences around the world.

Discover more mischief at **mischiefcomedy.com**

Follow us and be social

@mischiefcomedy

PETER PAN GOES WRONG

MISCHIEF MOVIE NIGHT

FOR MISCHIEF WORLDWIDE LTD

Directors	Mark Bentley, Jo Danvers, Henry Lewis, Jonathan Sayer, Hilary Strong (Chair), Kenny Wax
CEO	Jo Danvers
Head of Marketing & Brand	Harry Lockyear
Head of Licensing	Jessica Hall
Licensing Coordinator	Dorothy Oehmler
Marketing Coordinator	Nathan Garwood
Licensing & Brand Assistant	Jack Cowdery
Executive Assistant	Kae Deller
Consultant Financial Director	Charlotte Johnson
Bookkeeper	Jai Tosniwal

For all Mischief literary & replica rights enquiries please visit www.mischiefworldwide.com

Thespians

Cast

Thespis *(doubles with Rhodes Lead & Naxos backing)*
Poly *(doubles with chorus member 3, Crete & Thebes backing)*
Adonis *(doubles with Rhodes backing and Grecian 2)*
Melampus *(doubles with Chorus Leader, Crete & Thebes backing)*
Atlas *(doubles with chorus member 4, Rhodes backing)*
The Tyrant *(doubles with chorus member 5 and Grecian)*
Rhapsodes – *(plays Advisor One, Newsvendor, Messenger One, Angela Athena (Newsreader Two), Hera, Builder One, Crete Crooner, Thebes Two, Stage Manager, Dawn, Chat Show Host, Claire, Audience Member One, Mill House Guard)*
Bard – *(plays Advisor Two, Archimedes, Messenger Two, Greek Ern (Newsreader), Zeus, Builder Two, Rhodes (Bacchus Boy), Thebes One, Spike, Keith, Audience Member Two, Mill House Guard, Very Old Guard)*

All company play various Grecians at the start.

UNDERSTUDIES play chorus at various points (Grecians, performers in the Dionysia adoring fans, etc., and old men).

Setting

ANCIENT GREECE 534 BC

The Island of Ikaria and the Capital of Athens.

Terminology

MILL HOUSE – An Ancient Greek Prison.
DIONYSUS – God of Grape and Wine.
DIONYSIA – A large festival/competition held in honour of the god Dionysus

Please note: This text went to press before the first performance and so may slightly differ from the play as performed.

Act One

I. Prologue

Overture. Music plays, dramatic and intense. A tight light comes up on **Bard**, **Rhapsody** *as a Greek chorus.*

Rhapsodes Welcome all.

Bard Khaírete!

Rhapsodes We are the Greek chorus.

Dating back to the fifth century the chorus was made up of several hundred people!

Bard However for budgetary reasons this evening we are a chorus of two.

Rhapsodes Tonight's show will tell the story of how theatre was invented.

Bard This is a story of love. Of comedy.

Rhapsodes And some tragedy too.

Bard Not to mention some terrible puns.

Rhapsodes It's a tale of mistaken identity, humour and hubris . . .

Bard And other words beginning with H.

Rhapsodes . . . A haberdashery . . .

Bard Of one man's attempt to appease the gods by portraying them.

Lights up on **Thespis**.

Rhapsodes And how he would lose his friends by betraying them.

Bard Of his ambition . . .

Rhapsodes And his lover.

Lights up on **Atlas**.

Bard A grieving sister who goes undercover.

Lights up on **Poly**.

Rhapsodes Of a woman charged with an island's survival!

Bard And those who would end as our heroes' rival.

Lights up on **Adonis** *and* **Tyrant**.

Rhapsodes And hundreds of side characters played by us.

(*Pointing at* **Bard**.) Bard.

Bard (*pointing at* **Rhapsodes**) And Rhapsodes.

Rhapsodes Look out for his portrayal of nervous advisor in the opening. It's particularly good.

Bard Thanks. I use a Spanish accent.

Beat.

Rhapsodes Alright . . . But to tell this story as best we can, we must start from the beginning.

Bard Greece is the word.

Rhapsodes Ancient Greece, to be specific.

Bard On the tiny island of Ikaria.

Rhapsodes Where a dreadful drought had ravaged the land.

Bard You could say life was a load of A*crap*olis.

Rim shot.

Rhapsodes We did warn you. Terrible puns.

Bard This anguish can only be ended by appeasing the god Dionysus.

Rhapsodes Through a unified prayer sung to the heavens.

Bard And so we join our characters.

Rhapsodes At the height of their pain.

Rhapsodes As on bended knee they pray for rain . . .

Bard As on bended knee they pray for drizzle . . .

Lights shift and we are in a small, crumbling temple on the sleepy Grecian island of Ikaria (534 BC). The **Chorus** *become the* **Ikarians**.

Ikarians
OH DIONYSUS END OUR PAIN
END THIS CRISIS SEND US RAIN!
HEAR OUR CRIES
AND SEND US RAIN.

Beat. Huge musical shift. Upbeat, gospel.

RAIN
RAIN!
RAIN!!

Rhapsodes *enters as* **Newsvendor**.

Newsvendor Extra! Extra! Read all about it! Drought rages on! Read all about it in *The Daily Exposition*!

Melampus
IT'S BEEN FIVE LONG WEEKS
WE DON'T KNOW HOW LONG'S LEFT TO GO.

Adonis
IT'S HOTTER THAN HELL.

All
TSS!
AND DRIER THAN PINOT GRIGIO!

Atlas
WE'RE FED UP OF THIS FAMINE.

Ensemble Islanders
WE'RE TIRED OF THIS DROUGHT.

Melampus
THERE'S ONLY ONE WAY OUT!

Ikarians
DIONYSUS, END THIS
CRISIS, SEND US
WATER NOW!

DIONYSUS, END THIS
CRISIS, SEND US
WATER NOW!

Melampus
TEMPERATURE'S HIGH!

Ikarians
TEMPERATURE'S HIGH!

Melampus
TEMPERS ARE HIGHER!

Ikarians
TEMPERS ARE HIGHER!

Melampus
ALL THE CROPS DIE!

Ikarians
ALL THE CROPS DIE!

Melampus
IF THEY'RE NOT ON FIRE!

WE CAN'T GET BY.

Atlas
WE CAN'T GET DRIER!

Adonis
THE SITUATION'S GETTING SHIFTY.

Ikarians
WHACK ON EXTRA FACTOR 50!!

Melampus Keep praying, everyone.

Ikarians Yes, Melampus!

DIONYSUS, END THIS CRISIS,
SEND US WATER NOW!
DIONYSUS, END THIS CRISIS,
SEND US WATER NOW!

We transition to a grand palace in Athens. The **Tyrant** *is in 'the situation room' overwhelmed by bad news. She's surrounded by advisors (played by* **Bard** *and* **Rhapsodes***).*

Advisor One Your excellence, Crete is entirely out of water! Rhodes is in ruins.

Advisor Two (*with a Spanish accent*) And Santorini's run through its food supplies.

Tyrant Why do bad things happen to good dictators!

Advisor One They're all going to kill us!!

Tyrant (*light-bulb moment*) Not if they turn on each other first!

Advisors/Yes Men What?

Tyrant
WE'LL START A COMPETITION,
BETWEEN EACH COMMUNITY.

Advisors/Yes Men
YES!

Tyrant
WE'LL HOLD IT HERE IN ATHENS
IF THE AMPHITHEATRE'S FREE –

Advisors/Yes Men
YES YES!

Tyrant
THEY'LL ALL COMPETE BY PRAYING,
SO THEY WON'T BE ABLE TO SEE!

Advisor Two
SI!

Tyrant
THAT ALL THE TIME THEY'RE PRAYING
TAKES THE HEAT OFF ME!

Advisors/Yes Men
OO YES!

Tyrant
AND WITH EVERYONE THERE TOGETHER,
CHANTING IN ONE VOICE,
DIONYSUS WILL CHANGE THE WEATHER,
SHE'LL HAVE NO CHOICE!

All
DIONYSUS END THIS
CRISIS
SEND US WATER NOW!

Tyrant (*overlapping*)
OH YEAH!
OH YEAH!

Advisors/Yes Men
OO YEAH! YEAH! YEAH! YEAH!

Tyrant Zeus I'm good!

All
DIONYSUS
END THIS CRISIS
SEND US BUCKETLOADS'A
WA-TER
NOW . . .

Tyrant Sort the details! I'm off for my bath!

We're back in Ikaria. **Thespis** *and* **Poly** *wait at the chariot stop (***Pol** *laden with books). The music is suddenly full of optimism and promise.* **Thespis** *is carefree.* **Poly** *looks anxiously for their ride.*

Thespis Have you noticed the weather has been really good lately!?

Poly (*dead-pan*) Because it's a drought.

Thespis Just constantly glorious!

Poly (*dead-pan*) Because it's a drought.

Thespis Not a lot of water though?

Poly Because it's a . . . (*hits her face with a book*).

Thespis Pol, I'm clowning around, Zeus you're such an ancient Greek! Put your books away and look around. New ideas are being thought up every minute! Democracy, medicine! Yoghurt! And Archimedes has almost cracked the wheel.

Archimedes *(played by* **Bard***) pushes a large square wheel across the stage behind them.*

Archimedes I'M STILL WORKING ON IT!

Poly Have you thought about making it round?

Archimedes Nah! **Thespis** Nah!

Thespis One day I'm going to come up with something that means I won't just be known as Elder Leon's little kid anymore. I'll be famous and live in . . .

Poly Not this again!

Thespis
ATHENS!
SHINY, SPARKLY, ATHENS!

Poly Zeus!

Thespis
STIMULATING ATHENS.

IT'S A CITY FULL OF CHANCES,
FOR THOSE BRAVE ENOUGH TO TRY.

WHERE THE MODERN WORLD ADVANCES
AND THE TEMPLES TOUCH THE SKY!

AND CARVED IN THE STONES AND MARBLES,
ARE THE NAMES OF THE SPECIAL FEW,
WHO PAVED THE WAY,
WHO SAVED THE DAY,
WHO ARE HEROES,
THROUGH AND THROUGH!

AND ONE DAY MY NAME
WILL BE THERE TOO!
IN A(THENS) . . .

Poly
ATHENS.
YOU MEAN:
DIRTY, DATED, ATHENS!

Thespis Come on, sis!

Poly
OVERRATED ATHENS?

Thespis
SHINY, SPARKLY!

Poly
WHAT'S WRONG WITH HERE IN IKARIA?
THE NOBLEST ISLAND IN GREECE.

WE MAY NOT HAVE ARMIES,
LIKE RHODES OR CRETE,
WE MAY NOT HAVE CLEANERS
TO CLEAN THE STREET
WE MAY NOT HAVE WATER,
OR FOOD TO EAT . . .

BUT IT'S OUR HOME!
OUR SACRED HOME.

WE MAY BE LACKING IN
LITERALLY EVERYTHING,

BUT THERE'S SELDOM MUCH HARM,
FOR WHAT WE LACK IN RESOURCES
WE MAKE UP IN CHARM!

YES, I'M PROUD TO HAIL FROM IKARIA:
THE PLUCKIEST ISLAND IN GREECE!

Besides, how are you even going to get there? It's not like the Tyrant's just going to invite everyone over for wine and olives.

We jump between the different locations as the song builds pace. The **Tyrant** *is rolled across in a bath.*

Tyrant Prepare wine and olives! Send out a messenger across the land!

Poly Thespis, our chariot. Come on.

They start to run.

Newsvendor Extra! Extra! Tetchy Tyrant calls competition!

Things can only get Feta!

Tyrant
I LOVE TO THROW A PARTY!

A jazzy drum rhythm underscores the following section, as different groups speak their lines in rhythm and they build/overlap.

Adonis
RAIN GIVE US
RAIN GIVE US
RAIN GIVE US
RAIN NOW!

Atlas
PITTER PAT
PITTER PAT
TRICKLE TRICKLE
DROP DROP!

Adonis *and* **Atlas** *overlap as the* **Tyrant** *joins in on top.*

Adonis (*sotto voce*)
RAIN GIVE US
RAIN GIVE US
RAIN GIVE US
RAIN NOW!

RAIN GIVE US
RAIN GIVE US
RAIN GIVE US
RAIN NOW!

Atlas (*sotto voce*)
PITTER PAT
PITTER PAT
TRICKLE TRICKLE
DROP DROP!

PITTER PAT
PITTER PAT
TRICKLE TRICKLE
DROP DROP!

Tyrant
GOT SOME TROUBLES?
BATH WITH BUBBLES!

Melampus
SHOW(WER) –

Atlas
TRICKLE!

Melampus
– ER US . . .

Adonis
RAIN GIVE US
RAIN!

Melampus
. . . WITH RAIN!

Tyrant
BUBBLES!

Atlas
PITTER PAT!
PITTER PAT!

Melampus
SHOWER US . . .

Adonis
RAIN GIVE US
RAIN NOW!

Melampus
. . . WITH RAIN!

Tyrant
BUBBLES . . . BUBBLES!

Atlas
TRICKLE TRICKLE DROP!

Melampus
SHOWER US WITH RAIN!

Poly
COME ON
WE'VE GOT
TO GO!

Atlas
TRICKLE!

Adonis
RAIN GIVE US
RAIN

Thespis
TO ATHENS?

Poly
NO!

Tyrant
BUBBLES!

Poly
THESPIS LET'S GO . . .

Atlas
PITTER PAT
PITTER PAT

Melampus
SHOWER US
WITH RAIN

Adonis
RAIN GIVE US
RAIN NOW!

Atlas
TRICKLE
TRICKLE
DROP!

Tyrant
BUBBLES!

Thespis
ATHENS!

Tyrant
BUBBLES!

Adonis
RAIN GIVE US
RAIN GIVE US
RAIN GIVE US
RAIN NOW!

Atlas
PITTER PAT
PITTER PAT
TRICKLE TRICKLE
DROP DROP!

Melampus
SHOWER US WITH RAIN!

Tyrant
GOT TROUBLES?
BATH WITH BUBBLES!

Poly
THESPIS LET'S GO . . .

Thespis
ATHENS!

After building to a cacophony they all shout their lines in groups one after the other in increasing frenzy (the **Ikarians** *shout their line in unison).*

Ikarians
RAIN!

Thespis
ATHENS!

Tyrant
BUBBLES!

Poly
GO!

Speeding up.

Ikarians
RAIN!

Thespis
ATHENS!

Tyrant
BUBBLES!

Poly
GO!

Ikarians
RAIN!

Thespis
ATHENS!

Tyrant
BUBBLES!

Poly
GO!

Ikarians
RAIN!

Thespis
ATHENS!

Tyrant
BUBBLES!

Poly
GO!

Ikarians
RAIN!

Thespis
ATHENS!

Tyrant
BUBBLES!

Poly
GO!

All
OOOHHH!

DIONYSUS!
END THIS CRISIS!
SEND US WATER NOW!

Tyrant Give me water yummy now!

Poly *and* **Thespis** *are running to the temple.*

Poly Come on, we're almost there!

All

DIONYSUS,
SEND US RAINFALL
LET THE RAIN FALL DOWN!

The **Ikarians** *on their knees.*

All

SHOWER US WITH RAIN,
SHOWER US WITH WATER,
LET US LIVE AGAIN!

Poly *and* **Thespis** *running as the islanders pray. The* **Tyrant** *is wheeled across stage in a bubble bath by her* **Advisors**.

All

SEND US BUCKET LOADS'A WA –

TER –

NOW!!

(*shout*) OH DIONYSUS,
SEND RAIN!

II. The Temple

In the temple **Melampus**, **Atlas** *and* **Adonis** *are knelt in worship.*

Adonis Where are Thespis and Poly?!

Melampus Stop belly aching, Adonis, and get back to prayer.

Atlas Yes, Elder Melampus!

He falls to his knees in prayer.

Adonis We all know it only works if we're all here.

Melampus Zip it. I'm island Elder.

Adonis And I'm deputy Elder.

Melampus There is no such thing, Adonis!

Atlas Come on everyone! Where's the Ikarian *can do* spirit? Remember island rule two! *In times of drought there's only one way out!*

Melampus And that is to pray and sacrifice one of Atlas' goats.

Atlas But I have no more goats left?

Melampus Then we'll kill your cat.

Atlas Not Oedipuspus!

Adonis I should go in search of them. They may need to be rescued by a hero famed for playing by nobody's rules but his own.

Melampus There's only one thing of your own you're famed for playing with, Adonis.

Adonis It is my duty as head of the Ikarian army.

Melampus Ikaria does not have an army?

Adonis Then why did the men vote unanimously to make me their leader?

Melampus Who are these men?

Adonis That is secret.

Melampus Who is in the army?

Atlas Is it just you, Adonis?

Adonis That is also secret.

Melampus It's unlike Poly to be late for worship.

Adonis The same cannot be said for Thespis! He's a pain in my pythagor*ass*. He still owes me a silver coin.

Melampus Me too.

Atlas Me three. Remember it's a difficult day for them. It's a year since you know what.

Melampus Has it really been a year already?

Adonis Why can't he just be dependable like his sister. She lost her father too.

Melampus Because that's not who he is.

Atlas What do you mean, Melampus?

Music starts.

Melampus Thespis is not his sister in the same way I am not you and you are not me.

We cannot be who we are not, for we are who we are.

WE ARE WHO WE ARE

Melampus
I'M MONSTROUSLY OLD . . .

Adonis How old?

Melampus Fifty-two.

Atlas Wow!

Melampus (*sings*)
MY LIFE HAS BEEN STRUCK
BY ENDLESS BAD LUCK,
BUT WHAT CAN YA DO??

Atlas (*really concerned*) I don't know?

Melampus
I HAVE TO EMBRACE MY LOT,
I CANNOT BE WHAT I'M NOT!

I LIVE AS I LIVE
I DO WHAT I DO
I AM WHO I AM.

You see we're all stuck as ourselves for better or worse. Even the bits we don't like, we can't change.

Adonis Okay, thank you Melampus.

Melampus (*sings*)
I'M RIDDLED WITH PILES!

Adonis Oh, Zeus.

Melampus
MY BLOOD PRESSURE'S HIGH.
MY DIET IS POOR.
I'VE NO PELVIC FLOOR,
AND SOON I WILL DIE.

Atlas That's awful.

Melampus
BUT DARLING YOU HAVE TO SEE.
THESE THINGS ARE JUST PART OF ME.
I LIVE AS I LIVE,
IT'S GOT ME THIS FAR.

Atlas
YOU ARE WHO YOU ARE!

Melampus Now you're getting it, Atlas.

Atlas This is fun. May I have a try?

Melampus Of course.

Atlas (*sings*)
I FOLLOW THE RULES.
I DO AS I'M TOLD.
I'M SIMPLE AND PLAIN,
I STAY IN MY LANE;
STRIVE NOT TO BE BOLD!

I CANNOT GROW FACIAL HAIR.
I CRY WHEN THERE'S NO ONE THERE . . .

Moment of realisation. Snaps out of it.

BUT WHAT CAN I DO?
I DO WHAT I CAN
I AM WHO I AM.

Melampus Exactly, Atlas!

Adonis Haha! You're so weak and pathetic!

Melampus And he couldn't be any other way even if he tried.

Atlas (*happily*) I am a lost cause and I'm okay with it.

Melampus That's the spirit, Atlas.

Adonis Well, it's a good job I don't need to change.

Melampus Why, who are you?

Adonis Can't you see?

I AM A VERY STRONG MAN,
CALLED 'ADONIS THE GRAND MAN OF IKARIA'.
I'M A MUSCULAR MILITARY MAN

Erm. That's not right. The alliteration undermines me.

Again!

I AM A VERY STRONG MAN,
CALLED 'ADONIS THE GRAND MAN OF IKARIA'.

I AM WHO I AM,
I AM A MAN,

I AM WHO I AM.
I AM.

Melampus You've not understood the exercise, Adonis.

Atlas But, Melampus, why are we who we are?

Melampus What do you mean?

Atlas Why am I so meek? Why is Adonis so . . . unique? Why are we all so different? Why are you who you are?

Melampus It's down to what the fates have in store for us. Did I ever mention that I was once in love?

Adonis Yes. Yes, you have. **Atlas** Many times.

Melampus I ONCE HAD A LOVER.

Adonis There she goes.

Melampus
BUT NOW HE'S GONE.
FOR WHAT'S IN THE PAST,
IS IN THE PAST,
YOU MUST MOVE ON.

HE WAS THE MOST BEAUTIFUL SOLDIER,
HANDSOME WITH A BEARD
BUT ON THE DAY OF OUR WEDDING,
HE DISAPPEARED.

HE LEFT WITHOUT WARNING,
NO PARTING WORDS
AND LATER HIS FAMILY TOLD ME . . .
HE'D BEEN CARRIED AWAY BY A FLOCK OF BIRDS.

Adonis In the direction of the capital.	**Atlas** In the direction of the capital.

We know!

Melampus
BUT I HOLD ONTO THIS CHAIN,
IN THE HOPE OUR LOVE CAN THRIVE
THAT WE'LL ONE DAY MEET AGAIN.
IF HE'S EVEN STILL ALIVE . . .

Atlas (*gently*) Oh, Melampus.

Suddenly brighter. Peppy music.

IT IS WHAT IT IS!
DON'T CRY IN DESPAIR!

Adonis
AND AS YOU JUST SAID,
HE'S PROBABLY DEAD.
SO WHY EVEN CARE?

Atlas
AND THAT'S JUST THE WAY LIFE GOES.
YOU CAN'T WISH AWAY YOUR WOES.

Melampus
HE'S OUT OF MY LIFE.

Atlas Yes, Melampus!

I'M SPINELESS AND WEAK.

Melampus That's the spirit.

Adonis
I AM MAN!

Melampus Alright, Adonis . . .

Atlas
THERE'S NO POINT
IN HEROICS!

Melampus
TAKE A LESSON FROM THE STOICS!

All
I AM ME,
AND YOU ARE YOU;
THERE'S NOTHING MORE
THAT WE CAN DO.

Melampus	**Adonis**
FOR WE ARE!	FOR WE ARE!

Atlas

FOR WE ARE!

All

WHO

WE

ARE . . .

(Shouted.)
YEAH!

Poly *and* **Thespis** *enter.*

Poly I'm so sorry we're late everyone. I promise it will never happen again.

Melampus Right, back to prayer!

Thespis Morning friends! Melampus! Dehydration's looking good on you! Atlas, is that a miniature bust of one of the gods in your pocket or are you just pleased to see me!?

Atlas (*defensively*) It's a miniature bust! It's just a miniature bust.

Thespis And, Adonis, how's that sunburn doing, you big strong boy?

Slaps **Adonis** *on the back jovially.*

Adonis (*in pain*) I feel nothing. Thespis you must not disrespect me. I'm your deputy Elder.

Melampus No such thing!

Adonis And recently promoted head of the island's military.

Poly Congratulations! Before you were nonsense. Now you are general nonsense.

Adonis Haha. Very funny, Poly.

THE MESSAGE

A loud and important fanfare sounds.

Atlas Athenian messengers!

Two **Messengers** *(played by* **Rhapsodes** *and* **Bard***) enter in Athenian armour.*

Messenger One I am Achilles. Messenger and soldier to the Tyrant. Known for my valour and named after my weak heel.

Messenger Two I am his cousin Peenichilles . . . I also have a weak heel.

Music plays.

Messengers One & Two
WE COME BEARING NEWS FROM THE TYRANT
WE COME WITH THE TYRANT'S DECREE.

Messenger One
AND, ONCE IT'S BEEN COMPLETED –

Messenger Two
IT CANNOT BE REPEATED!

Messengers One & Two
SO LISTEN VERY CAREFULLY.

Messenger One *(clears throat)*
THE TYRANT IS TO HOLD A COMPETITION
IT'S OBLIGATORY THAT EVERY TOWN TAKE PART.

Messenger Two
T'WILL BE HELD AT THE AMPHITHEATRE . . .
IN ATHENS.

Thespis *(coming to life)* Athens!

Messenger One
DOORS AT 7 FOR A 7.30 START.

Messenger Two
EACH PROVINCE WILL PRESENT A PRAYER
CHANTED IN ONE BREATH.
THE BEST WILL WIN IT,
FAIR AND SQUARE.

Messengers One & Two
THE LOSERS PUT TO DEATH.

Messengers One
TO NOT TAKE PART,
IS A PUNISHABLE CRIME.

Messengers One & Two
AND THE GAMES SHALL START,
IN FIVE DAYS' TIME.

ANY QUESTIONS?

Melampus We're all done for!

Adonis I say we kill them both!

Melampus It's not a bad idea! Pretend they never reached us.

Melampus *draws a bow and arrow and points at* **Messenger Two**. **Messenger One** *points his arrow at* **Melampus**.

Messenger Two Don't shoot the messenger.

Beat.

Poly Have you all lost your minds?

Thespis Pol's right. Can't you all see? This is great news! Athenian friends, tell the Tyrant that the island of Ikaria accepts her invitation!

Messenger One It's not really an RSVP kind of vibe . . .

Messenger Two More of a command on pain of execution.

Thespis Then tell her . . . Er . . . Er . . . Tell her we've written a new prayer!

Everyone is shocked. Optimistic music bubbles, etc.

Melampus Thespis –

Poly What are you saying!?

Thespis (*going into dream world*) It's going to wow the capital –

Adonis Thespis –

Thespis You're right, Adonis. It's going to wow the world! I can see the headlines now! 'Thespis dazzles with daring *prayer-ring*!'

Adonis What are you doing?

Thespis

IT'S A PRAYER WITH HEART AND FEELING,
UNLIKE ANY HEARD BEFORE!

IT'LL LEAVE THE TYRANT REELING,
AND THEN SHOUTING OUT FOR MORE!

He shouts enthusiastically. The others try to get him to stop.

SO, TELL THOSE FOLKS IN ATHENS
BEFORE THE GAMES BEGIN –
THAT COMING THERE'S A SPECIAL PRAYER,
THE BEST THERE'S EVER BEEN!
YES, WE'VE GOT THE PRAYER
THAT'S GOING TO WIN!

IN . . .
ATHENS!
TITILLATING ATHENS!
AWE-INSPIRING ATHENS!
WHERE I'M OFF TO MAKE MY NAME
WIN AWARDS AND LIVE IN FAME!
AND WRITE A PRAYER
THAT SETS THE TOWN AGLOW.

Approaches **Messenger**.

SO, JUST BE A LOVE,
AND LET THE TYRANT KNOW?

Beat.

Messenger One (*smitten*) We'll tell her you're very attractive, I mean, confident.

Thespis And don't forget to mention my name. Thespis!

Messenger Two You have five days.

Messengers One & Two
LONG LIVE THE TYRANT.
LONG LIVE THE TYRANT.

LONG LIVE
THY
TY –
RANT.

BYE!

They exit.

Adonis Oh, figs!

Melampus Zeus what have you done, Thespis!? A whole new prayer.

Poly In five days!

Melampus Poseidon's backstroke! I'm having a vision!

(*In a trance.*) Arghrarararaooo!!! This competition shall change everything.

NOTHING WILL BE THE SAME AGAIN!
I SEE JOY, I SEE PAIN, I SEE REGRET.

Adonis How extraordinarily unspecific!

Melampus I see more!

ADONIS SHALL BE HUMILIATED
BEFORE SUNSET.

Atlas Poor Adonis, Melampus is never wrong!

Adonis Yes she is! She's always wrong!

Atlas What are we doing to do?

Poly We must try and write something! Does anyone have papyrus and pen?

Melampus Young people and their technology!

What's wrong with the old-fashioned way of writing things? To score it into the skin of an inferior man with a knife?

That reminds me, Atlas, show me my to-do list for the day.

Atlas Yes, Melampus.

Atlas *rips open his shirt to reveal the words 'SHARPEN KNIFE' on his torso.*

Thespis Please! Don't you see, this is a great opportunity! To put Ikaria on the map and for me to finally go to live in

Music spikes.

ATHENS!
SPARKLY, SHINY –

Melampus Enough, Thespis. You're not going to Athens.

Thespis What do you mean?

Melampus You will remain in Ikaria! I'm afraid it's too much of a risk!

Thespis But, Melampus –

Melampus Your father, Zeus rest his soul, put me in charge of this island and I have to do what's best for everyone. Now who will volunteer to write a new prayer for us?

Adonis *puts his hand up.*

Adonis Oh!!

Melampus Anyone? Anyone at all?

Adonis Me!

Looks pleadingly at **Poly**.

Melampus Someone smart and good with words? Poly?

Poly *looks away, terrified. Beat.*

Melampus . . . Very well . . . Adonis. You will write our prayer.

Adonis Yes!

Thespis This is so unfair, Melampus! You're killing my dream!

He runs off.

Atlas I'll get him.

He runs off.

Adonis When the island asks for a miracle, Adonis the Grand Man of Ikaria answers and his answer is hello, I am the miracle you were looking for, hi, how are you? Family keeping well . . .? Farewell beta people! I have muscles to oil, a prayer to write and a people to save!!

Melampus *pulls* **Adonis'** *robe down to his ankles.*

Adonis WHAT ARE YOU DOING?!

Melampus Melampus is always right.

He exits. **Poly** *and* **Melampus** *are left alone.*

Melampus Oh Poly, why didn't you put your hand up?

Poly I'm not really an ideas person, Lampy.

Melampus You're always coming up with ideas! The alarm clock, the crane and what about that sketch you showed me with all the clever underground tubes that transport water around the town?

Poly It's just a pipe dream.

Melampus You know full well you're the smartest person on the island by a Greek mile.

Poly Not much of a flex is it? There's only seven of us and one's Adonis.

Melampus Pol, I know it's a difficult time but . . . I see so much of him in you.

Poly Adonis?

Melampus Your father. When times were tough we looked to him. And now we need you. Don't you want to be a hero like the characters in your books?

Poly I'm nothing like them. They're all so, you know, 'WOAH' and I'm so sort of 'eeeergh'.

<u>THE GIRL WHO KNOWS EVERYTHING</u>

WHO WOULDN'T WANT TO BE ONE OF THEM?
THOSE INCREDIBLE IDOLS OF GREECE!

THERE'S ARACHNE WHO CHALLENGED
AND GOADED THE GODS
OR MYRINA WHO FOUGHT
AGAINST ALL OF THE ODDS
THEN CRUSHED ALL HER FOES
WITH HER MUSCULAR QUADS!

BUT WHAT AM I?
WELL . . .
I'M THE GIRL WHO KNOWS EVERYTHING!

CLEVER AND QUICK
AND RELIABLE
THE MOST CAPABLE
PERSON IN TOWN

'THAT POLY WHO COLDLY
RECITES BY ROTE
THE GREAT GRECIAN THINKERS AND
ALL THAT THEY WROTE
YES SHE'S ALWAYS ON HAND WITH A
QUIP OR QUOTE'

SHE'S THE GIRL WHO HAS TO KNOW
EVERYTHING!

SO SHE TRAWLS THROUGH THE STORIES
THAT SHE FINDS ON HER SHELF
TO FIND IN HER HEROES
WHAT SHE LACKS HERSELF

AND THAT CAPABLE GIRL FROM IKARIA
IS LEFT IN A TERRIBLE TIZZ,
FOR THE GIRL WHO KNOWS EVERYTHING
HASN'T A CLUE WHO SHE IS . . .

Melampus I do, Pol. And soon you will. Come, let's go for a walk.

She exits.

Poly

BUT SHE DOES WANT TO KNOW,
AND SHE DOES WANT TO FEEL
AND SHE DOES WANT TO FOLLOW HER CALL . . .
THE GIRL WHO KNOWS EVERYTHING AND NOTHING AT ALL
THE GIRL WHO KNOWS EVERYTHING AND NOTHING AT ALL

AND HOW COULD YOU EVER GET CLOSE TO HER?
THE GIRL WHO LIVES MILES AWAY!
WHOSE DEEPEST OF FEELINGS REMAIN UNSAID,
WHO RETREATS TO THE SAFETY OF STORIES INSTEAD,
AND REPLACES THE WORLD WITH THE WORLD IN HER HEAD
SHE'S THE GIRL WHO KNOWS NOTHING AT ALL!

BUT SHE HAS SO MUCH TO GIVE
AND SO MUCH TO SAY
AND SO MUCH TO BE
IF SHE JUST FOUND A WAY

BUT DEEP DOWN SHE KNOWS
IF SHE WANTS TO KNOW MORE
SHE MUST PUT DOWN THE BOOKS
AND THEN OPEN THE DOOR

AND STEP OUT AS SOMEBODY NEW
JUST AS HER IDOLS WOULD DO.
AND SHE DOES HAVE A FEELING
THAT A NEW GIRL COULD BE,
WELL, JUST ROUND THE CORNER . . .

A sudden thought occurs.

IN ATHENS?!
LET'S SEE . . .
AND THAT CAPABLE GIRL FROM IKARIA
COULD ESCAPE FROM HER TERRIBLE TIZZ
WHEN THE GIRL WHO KNOWS

EVERYTHING FINALLY KNOWS
WHO POLY IS!

III. The Coast

Atlas Thespis, wait!

Thespis Leave me alone, Atlas.

Atlas You can't just run off during prayer! Remember Island Rule eighteen.

Thespis Will you stop banging on about the rules!?

Atlas I can't! Island rule number seventy-two is to never stop banging on about the rules.

Thespis And where's that got you!? You're vocally hoarse, with scabby knees. You're a slip of a man.

Atlas We can't all be like you. A free thinker and a bad boy. With the mind of Athena and the thighs of Zeus.

Thespis What?

Atlas Nothing. Oh, Thespis, what are you going to do?

Thespis . . . I'm still going to Athens but I'm going alone!

Atlas OMZ! Thespis, you can't!

Thespis Why not?

Atlas It's dangerous! It's forbidden!

Thespis Atlas, can you imagine what it's like to have the one thing you want more than anything right in front of you and the only thing that's stopping you from taking it, is fear?

Atlas I don't think so.

Music plays. Hopeful and uplifting.

Thespis Then try! Because there's a whole world out there.

Another musical spike.

Where nobody says, 'There goes Elder Leon's disappointing son'. Just think, a fresh start.

Music plays again.

WORLD OUT THERE

THERE'S A WORLD OUT THERE, ATLAS.
THERE'S A WORLD OUT THERE.
JUST SITTING THERE, WAITING FOR ME.

A WORLD OUT THERE,
A WHOLE WORLD OUT THERE,
FAR BEYOND THE IKARIAN SEA.

THERE ARE PLACES I'M APPLAUDED
THE SECOND I APPEAR.
WHERE I'M GLORIFIED AND LAUDED,
FOR SIMPLY BEING NEAR.
IF YOU LISTEN
YOU CAN HEAR IT IN THE AIR:
'WOO!'
THERE'S A WORLD OUT THERE!

Atlas I can't hear anything.

Thespis

THERE'S A WORLD OUT THERE. LISTEN!
HEAR THE WORLD OUT THERE!
A MAGIC WORLD, SQUINT AND YOU'LL SEE.
TAKE A PROPER STARE, 'CAUSE THAT WORLD OUT THERE.
IS WHERE I AM DESTINED TO BE.

ALL THE PARTIES THAT I'M HOSTING
ARE GLAMOROUS AND GRAND.
AND AT WEEKENDS I'M THERE TOASTING
WITH THE LEADERS OF THE LAND.
I HAVE POWER, WEALTH AND INFLUENCE TO SPARE.
IN MY WORLD OUT –

Atlas
HOLD ON, THESPIS, HAVE YOU THOUGHT THIS THROUGH?

Thespis
I HAVE!

Atlas
HAVE YOU REALLY THOUGHT THIS THROUGH?

Thespis
OF COURSE. WELL SORT OF . . .

Atlas
HMMM.

Thespis
BUT . . .

Atlas
CHANGE LIKE THAT REQUIRES THINKING THROUGH.

Thespis
I KNOW.

Atlas
ARE YOU REALLY SO SURE
THAT'S THE RIGHT THING TO DO?

Thespis Atlas! Have you never thought about a better life for yourself?

Atlas I've never really thought about myself at all. Island rule forty-one there's no I in Island.

Thespis Forget the stupid rules for a second. Look out on the horizon and tell me what you see for *yourself.*

Atlas Okay, Erm . . .

He tries to see his future.

THERE'S A WORLD OUT THERE.
A WHOLE WORLD OUT THERE . . .

MAYBE . . . THERE COULD BE
. . . SAND.

Thespis Right.

Atlas
THERE'S A WORLD OUT THERE.

Thespis Zeus!

Atlas
A WHOLE WORLD OUT THERE.
ERM . . . YES, MAYBE I THINK THERE IS SAND.

IT'S A WORLD WHERE I AM NOTICED.
A WORLD THAT'S NOT SO BAD.
WHERE MY GOATS AREN'T ALWAYS KILLED
AND I'M NOT USED AS A NOTEPAD.

LIFE WOULDN'T JUST BE SOMETHING TO
WITHSTAND.
AND THERE'S PROBABLY . . .
SAND.

Thespis See. Feels pretty good right?

Atlas No! Thespis. There are rules for a reason and the grapes aren't always greener on the other side!

THERE'S A WORLD RIGHT HERE, THESPIS
YOU'VE A HOME RIGHT HERE.
WITH YOUR FAMILY, YOUR TRIBE,
THE FRIENDS WHO LOVE YOU . . .
SO STAY, THESPIS, STAY.

Thespis
BUT I WANT TO SEE THE WORLD!

Atlas
THESPIS STAY!

Thespis
I HAVE TO SEE THE WORLD!
THE WORLD OUT THERE!

Lyrics start to overlap, etc.

Atlas
THERE'S A WORLD THAT'S RIGHT IN FRONT OF YOU.
ALL YOU'LL EVER NEED IS HERE.

Thespis
OUT THERE.

Atlas
STAY! LOOK AT WHAT'S AROUND YOU.

Thespis
BUT THERE –

Atlas
STAY HERE.
STAY, THESPIS, STAY.

Thespis
SO BY THIS TIME TOMORROW
I'LL LEAVE IKARIA BEHIND!
I'LL STEAL A BOAT
AND SAIL ACROSS THE SEA!

Atlas This is mad!

Thespis
NO MORE DISAPPOINTED GLANCES,
OR FINAL SECOND CHANCES,
I WON'T BE MY FATHER'S SON,
I'LL JUST BE ME!

Atlas
BUT THIS IS WHERE YOU'RE MEANT TO BE.
WE NEED YOU HERE!

Thespis
YOU REALLY DON'T.

Atlas
WE NEED YOU HERE.

Thespis
BUT WHY?

Atlas
I NEED YOU HERE!

Thespis *is shocked.*

Atlas I mean . . . the truth is I . . . I mean to say that I . . . that we all need you here.

Thespis Like who?

Atlas What about Poly?

Thespis What about her?

Atlas She's lost her dad too and now she'd lose a brother.

Thespis She'll be fine. Pol doesn't have emotions. She just reads books.

Atlas Maybe that's her way of coping.

Put yourself in her sandals for a moment.

Musical sting.

Thespis What do you mean?

Atlas Well, when I'm trying to understand someone else's point of view or how they're feeling, I imagine myself as them, wearing their sandals; inhabiting their life and suddenly I know them completely.

Musical sting.

Thespis Incredible . . .

Atlas If we were able to exist as one another for a day I imagine the world would be a much better place.

Thespis That's it! Oh, Atlas you're a genius!

Atlas What do you mean?

Thespis
IF WE JUST WEAR EACH OTHERS' . . .

Atlas What?!

Thespis
THEN WE COULD . . .
YES! AND SAVE THE DAY!

WHICH MEANS THAT . . .

Atlas Backup, Thespis . . .

Thespis
GO TO ATHENS!

Atlas
WHAT ARE YOU TRYING TO SAY?

Thespis
I'M SAYING YOU'RE AMAZING, ATLAS!

Atlas *gasps and blushes.*

Atlas Mahh!

Thespis
AND I WAS FOOLISH NOT TO SEE
THAT THERE'S A WORLD JUST WAITING HERE!

Atlas
YOU THINK THAT I'M AMAZING?

Thespis
AND WHAT JOY IT'S GOING TO BE
TO SHOW THAT WORLD OUR NEW IDEA.

Atlas
WELL, I THINK YOU'RE AMAZING TOO!

Thespis
THERE'S A WORLD OUT THERE.

Thespis *looks across the sea,* **Atlas** *looks at* **Thespis**.

Thespis
RIGHT HERE.

Atlas
RIGHT HERE!

Thespis *runs off.* **Atlas** *follows.*

IV. Back at the Temple (Into Rehearsals)

Poly, **Melampus** *and other islanders stand in a semi-circle watching* **Adonis**. *An irregular drumbeat starts. (Courtesy of* **Bard** *and* **Rhapsodes***).*

Adonis
THE DROUGHT IS LONG.
MY THIGHS ARE STRONG.
OH GODS, GIVE US RAIN.
MY ARMS ARE STRONG.
OH GODS GIVE US RAIN.
MY THIGHS
AND ARMS ARE STRONG!
ARE STRONG!

Adonis *ends in a heroic position.*

Poly Oh shit.

Thespis *and* **Atlas** *arrive.*

Thespis Everyone. I've got it!

Poly Thespis! Where've you been all night? I've been worried sick.

Thespis I'm sorry Pol, but I have an idea for the competition. Well, it's Atlas' really.

Melampus Thespis, I have made my decision.

Adonis Besides you're too late. I have just unveiled my masterpiece.

Poly He rhymed strong with strong.

Thespis Listen! We all need to wear each others' sandals!

Adonis Your big idea is a shoe swap! How will that help?

Thespis Just watch!

He starts to act.

I am Dionysus, god of grape and wine.

Melampus What are you doing?

Thespis I'm acting . . . It's saying and being someone who you are not by living in their sandals. Who's this? I'm the kindest man on the island. I worry about everyone except for myself and I know all the island rules by heart.

Atlas Haha! He is meus!

Thespis Every day Boulia Melampus takes my figs and tells me to spend an extra hour praying to Dionysus whilst she sleeps with my Dadius.

Melampus Haha! He's added a fictional element to the character for dramatic effect. Very good, Thespis.

Poly This is so clever.

Atlas Do another!

Thespis Okay. I'm so muscular! Every morning I stuff my loincloth full of apples so I look more well-endowed.

Adonis I have no idea who that could be.

Two apples fall out of his robe.

It must be apple season!

Melampus Look, I'll concede this is most novel, but what does this have to do with our prayer?

Thespis That's it, Melampus! Acting shall be our prayer! Imagine. We each portray a different character and tell the audience a story.

Atlas How thrilling!

Thespis We're sure to delight the Tyrant and win the Dionsyia! Nobody will have seen anything like it!

Poly What of the gods? Surely we must think of the story of Capeneus!

Everyone nods along. Hmmm, yes, etc.

Poly I mean, will we not anger them?

Thespis Fear not! We shall present their side of the story too. The gods will be flattered.

Poly What do you think, Elder Melampus?

Melampus WOAH!!!!

Melampus *goes into a trance. Music plays.*

I SEE A WORLD AWAY FROM THIS ISLAND.
ONE OF FAME, RICHES AND SUCCESS.

Thespis Then it's settled.

Melampus In the future many will try acting. There will be things called plays and they will tell the stories of kings and queens and of love and loss. There will even be a play where everyone is a cat and there will be no discernible plot and yet it will prove very popular.

Music cuts out.

But I also see . . .

Music starts.

THAT IN MANY WAYS WE WIN,
BUT IN OTHERS WE WILL FAIL,
FOR MERGED WITH OUR SUCCESS,
IS UNHAPPINESS AND BETRAYAL.

Atlas How can there be unhappiness in a life of fortune?

Melampus

PRIDE LEADS US TO ANGUISH,
AND TAKES VICTORY AWAY,
AND ONLY TRUE LOVE'S GIFT,
CAN EVER SAVE THE DAY.

Adonis Oh, please!

Music cuts out.

Melampus Oh and Adonis shall die by the arrow of an Athenian soldier.

Adonis You don't frighten me.

Melampus Boo.

Adonis *shrieks and many apples drop from his robe.*

Adonis What an apple season we're having!

Thespis Can we try, Melampus?

Melampus I don't know, Thespis.

Poly It's either that or we sail across the sea to sing only of Adonis' thighs.

Adonis (*sincere*) Ah, a conundrum.

Poly Think about the tale of Odysseus. He had to choose between sailing his ship into a giant whirlpool that would certainly kill everyone on board or sail his ship into a six-headed monster that was only very likely to kill everyone on board.

Thespis Thanks for the vote of confidence, Pol.

Poly I'm saying the odds are in your favour, Thespis.

Atlas And Melampus did say that if we try 'acting' we'd have great success.

Adonis She also said that there would be unhappiness, betrayal and that I would be shot with an arrow.

Poly I guess we'll have to deal with that as and when it happens. We don't have anything to lose!

Atlas I'm in!

Puts his hand in.

Melampus I'm in.

Puts her hand in.

Adonis Fine.

Puts his hand in.

Melampus Then it's settled . . .

<u>THE REHEARSAL</u>

Music starts.

Melampus Over to you, Thespis. Tell us what do to.

Thespis Well, first of all we need to warm up. Clear the space! Make a circle . . .

Everyone stands in a circle. **Thespis** *claps.*

ZIP.

Poly What was that?

Thespis It's how you prepare to act. We pass this clap around in a circle.

Adonis How does that help?

Thespis Just give it go.

Everyone passes the clap round the circle.

Thespis
ZIP.

Melampus
ZIP.

Adonis
ZIP.

Atlas
ZIP.

Poly
ZIP.

Adonis
ZIP.

Thespis
NOW SHAKE IT OUT!

Thespis *shakes about. Everyone copies, confused.*

Poly Shake what out?

Thespis Now, everyone, stand in neutral.

Atlas What in the name of Zeus is neutral?

Thespis
IT'S THIS.

He stands oddly, chest forward. Everyone copies.

Poly Now can we start acting?

Thespis No! First we've got to warm up our mouths.

Melampus Dare I ask how we do that?

Thespis Like this!

THEY SAY WHEN YOU PASS
PAST THE PATH TO THE PARTHENON
PART OF THE PARTHENON
PASSES YOU BY.

Now you try!

Thespis *gestures for everyone to repeat. They are not very good! It's all a bit out of time and off pitch.*

Everyone
THEY SAY WHEN YOU PASS
PAST THE PATH TO THE PARTHENON
PART OF THE PARTHENON
PASSES YOU BY.

Thespis Close enough . . .

LA LA LA LA

Everyone
LA LA LA LA!

Melampus Enough! The Dionysia is four days away. Let's begin!

Thespis But we need to do trust falls.

Adonis CATCH ME!

Melampus There's no time for that.

Adonis *falls backwards and hits the ground hard.*

Melampus Please, just teach me how to act.

Thespis Pick someone in the group to become and we'll try and work out who it is.

Melampus *stands in front of her peers.*

Melampus (*woodenly*)
I AM MELAMPUS ACTING.
I AM ACTING AS ATLAS.
I AM MELAMPUS CAN YOU GUESS WHO I AM?

Beat.

Thespis No. You can't just say who you are. You have to become the person.

Melampus But how do I do that!?

Poly You need to break it down a little, Thespis.

Music starts.

Thespis Well, I suppose I look at the person . . . and I think about their life.

I WATCH HOW THEY WALK.
SEE HOW THEY STAND.
HEAR HOW THEY TALK,
AND TRY TO UNDERSTAND,

Melampus Understand what?

Thespis
HOW IT FEELS TO BE THEM
ON JUST A REGULAR DAY.
WHAT MAKES THEM LAUGH,
WHAT KIND OF THINGS THEY SAY.

TRY TO LOOK IN,
WHAT'S ON THEIR MIND,
UNDER THE SKIN,
WHAT DO YOU FIND?

Puts his arm around **Atlas**. **Atlas** *looks on lovingly.*

Thespis
TRY TO IMAGINE PROBLEMS
MORE LIKE HIS.

YOU ACT LIKE HIM,
SHE ACTS LIKE YOU.
THAT'S WHAT ACTING IS.

Melampus Aha! I think I get it! How about this.

MY NAME IS ATLAS,
MY LIFE IS RUBBISH.
I WANT MY LIFE TO SHINE
AND GLOW, BUT NO.
IT'S RUBBISH.

WHEN I MEET MELAMPUS
I TRY AND GRIN.
AS SHE WRITES HER SCHEDULE
ON MY SKIN.

MUST SHE USE THAT KNIFE?
OH ZEUS MY LIFE . . .
IS RUBBISH.

Beat. Everyone claps.

Poly That was brilliant, Melampus!

Melampus I feel dreadful! My heart is aching.

Thespis That's because you felt what it was like to be Atlas.

Melampus It's awful! Atlas I'm so sorry for how I've treated you.

Atlas That's okay, Melampus.

Melampus No, it's not. From now on I swear by the tip of Olympus to treat you better.

Poly Thespis this is amazing! Can I have a go?

Thespis The stage is waiting, Pol!

Poly I was thinking I could do some background reading first, maybe something from the works of Miletus perhaps?

Thespis Pol, this isn't something you can learn from a book. Just dive in and trust yourself.

Poly Okay . . .

She steps forward.

WOAH!!
MY NAME'S MELAMPUS,
I AM QUITE OLD . . .
WHICH MEANS I WORRY
EVERY TIME I CATCH A COLD.

Thespis What about how she feels?

Something clicks.

Poly
I ONCE HAD A LOVER,
BUT WHERE IS HE?

HOW SAD THAT THAT'S THE ONLY
THING I CAN'T FORESEE.

MY LIFE IS RUBBISH.

Everyone claps.

Poly Oh, Melampus. Your life's a chariot crash too! From now on I promise I'll always listen when you tell us about your soldier.

Melampus I feel seen!

They hug.

Adonis Ha! Your life is so depressing, Melampus.

Melampus I'll do another!

I'M A RIDICULOUS MAN,
THE STUPIDEST MAN IN IKARIA.
I'M AWKWARD AND PALE.
I'M LUSTFUL AND WEIRD.
I FREQUENTLY FAIL TO GROW A BEARD.
MY LIFE IS RUBBISH. RUBBISH! RUBBISH! *RUBBISH*
– (ETC.)

Adonis (*interrupting*) Alright! We get the point. My life is rubbish.

Everyone claps except **Adonis**.

Adonis Don't clap that.

It's my turn! Oooooh! Neutral!

I AM ADONIS,
I AM SO LONELY,
I WANT TO PROVE TO MY MOTHER
THAT I HAVE A PARTNER
AND ALSO I'M SEXUALLY ACTIVE.

I CRAVE HER APPROVAL!
I CRAVE HER LOVE!
I CRAVE LOVE.

Heavy pause.

Thespis Wow, Adonis. There's a lot to unpack there.

Adonis (*harrowed*) Nailed it!

Thespis Well done, cast! Almost everyone has made a lot of progress today. We start again first thing tomorrow.

Two **Newsreaders** *enter (***Bard** *and* **Rhapsodes***)*

Newsreader One Hello and welcome to the news at 9.

Newsreader Two I'm Angela Athena.

Newsreader One And I'm Greek Ern.

Newsreader Two And now for our headlines.

Newsreader One The first annual Dionysia is now only three days away and as pressure mounts things are truly hotting up.

Newsreader Two Meanwhile concern grows as Medea opens up new childcare facility.

Newsreader One Icarus is accused of nepotism as he gets too close to his son.

Newsreader Two And woman accused of getting lost after kidnapping a man with the head of a bull and the body of a man insists she was just taking a mina-de-tour.

Newsreader One And now for the sport.

Newsreader Two And now for the sport.

Everyone leaves. **Poly** *and* **Thespis** *hang back.*

Poly Thespis, if this is to be our prayer, shouldn't we work out what everyone will say?

Thespis Zeus, you're right.

Poly I could write something?

Thespis Really!?

Poly There's probably someone else who'd do a better job so just forget I said it.

Thespis No, Pol, please. I can't do this without you.

Beat. The two smile at each other. Seeing each other differently somehow.

Poly And, Thespis, I'm sorry.

Thespis Whatever for?

Poly
FOR NOT CUTTING YOU SLACK,
OR BELIEVING IN YOU.
AND SOMETIMES I FORGET YOU'VE LOST A FATHER TOO.

Thespis You reckon this will work?

Poly Did the Bellerophon slay the Chimera?

Thespis . . . I have no idea, Pol?

Everyone
I ACT LIKE YOU,
YOU ACT LIKE ME.
THAT'S WHAT ACTING . . .

Thespis Morning everyone! Today we're going to start looking at the text. Written by my amazing sister!

They clap and **Poly** *takes a little awkward bow.*

Thespis But first let's warm up.

Everyone
THEY SAY WHEN YOU PASS
PAST THE PATH TO THE PARTHENON
PART OF THE PARTHENON PASSES YOU BY.

Poly *looks to* **Thespis** *who gives her the nod. She runs to the front and takes charge.*

Poly Getting there but repeat after me.

WHEN YOU'VE PASSED PAST THE PATH TO THE PARTHENON.

Everyone
WHEN YOU'VE PASSED PAST THE PATH TO THE PARTHENON.

Poly
PART OF THE PARTHENON PASSES YOU BY.

Everyone
PART OF THE PARTHENON PASSES YOU BY.

Poly From the top!

Everyone
THEY SAY WHEN YOU PASS
PAST THE PATH TO THE PARTHENON
PART OF THE PARTHENON PASSES YOU BY.

Poly Very good!

Everyone
LA LA LA LA LA,
LA LA LA LA LA
LA . . .

Adonis Trust fall!

He falls backwards and crashes to the floor.

Poly Here's the scripts. Everyone take a copy.

Everyone reads.

Atlas Who's who?

Poly Yeah . . . We need someone who picks who plays which part? And tells everyone where to stand.

Adonis A dictator.

Poly A director.

Everyone looks to **Thespis**.

Thespis It shouldn't be me. We're a team.

(*Looks to* **Atlas** *subtly.*) Island rule forty-one.

Atlas A bad boy who knows the rules.

Thespis What?

Atlas Nothing. I was just thinking about . . . the rules.

Poly Melampus! You're our elder. Will you be our director too?

Melampus I couldn't, but I could . . . I mustn't! But I will.

She puts on a director's beret. **Poly** *passes her the script and she thumbs through the sides.*

Melampus (*unable to hide pleasure*) Gather round everyone, I will decide your parts.

(*To* **Poly**)
YOU BE THE GUARD –

Poly Yes, boss!

Melampus (*to* **Adonis**)
YOU BE THE ELDER.

Adonis
YES! FINALLY!

They all huddle around as **Melampus** *continues to cast everyone. Time jumps forward.*

Melampus Right, from the top!

Poly, **Melampus**, **Atlas** *and* **Adonis** *stand in front of everyone. Music shifts.*

Poly
WE'VE HAD NO RAIN FOR THIRTY DAYS.
I SEE NO END IN SIGHT.

Atlas (*timidly*)
WE KNEEL TO THE GODS AND GIVE THEM
PRAISE.

Adonis
MAN ENTERS FROM STAGE RIGHT!

Melampus Stop there.

Poly Adonis, that's not your line. That's a stage direction.

Melampus And, Atlas. You can be much louder. And, Poly, try . . . a regional accent. From the top. Again.

Poly (*in a strong regional accent*)
WE'VE HAD NO RAIN FOR THIRTY DAYS.
I SEE NO END IN SIGHT.

Atlas (*very loudly*)
WE KNEEL AND TO THE GODS GIVE PRAISE.

Adonis *enters the scene and delivers his line with his back to the audience.*

Adonis
I AM SO FULL OF FRIGHT.

Melampus No. That's wrong.

Adonis I agree. The line just doesn't really work, does it?

Thespis No. You need to face the audience, Adonis.

Adonis Of course. Of course. And what is an audience?

Melampus From the top!

Everyone
OPEN YOUR HEART,
OPEN YOUR MIND,
UNDER YOUR SKIN,
WHAT DO YOU FIND.

All make notes as if doing homework.

THAT'S WHAT ACTING IS . . .

We go to the top of Olympus. **Zeus** (**Bard**) *watches down on mankind with binoculars,* **Hera** (**Rhapsodes**) *stands next to him.*

Zeus What in the name of me are they doing down there? Hera! The mortals are doing impressions of us!

Hera Yeah, it's for the Dionysia.

Zeus The Dio what?

Hera Nysia. I knew you weren't listening. The competition in two days. You said we could go.

Zeus Well I've had a lot on my plate. Prometheus stole fire and I've chained him to a cliff so vultures can forever eat his liver.

Hera Why? You got issues, Zeus.

Zeus (*very upset*) Of course I have! When I was a child my father, Cronos god of heaven, tried to eat me! You can't just shrug that shit off.

Hera I'm going to bed. Don't forget to feed the cat.

She exits.

Zeus Unbelievable. Where's the bloody cat gone? Olympuspus? Where are you girl? Who wants some num nums?

They exit and we jump to **Melampus**.

Adonis Melampus. I was hoping you might help me. I worry that I'm letting everyone down.

Melampus Adonis, that's because you are letting everyone down. You are who you are!

Adonis But that's it! Maybe I could change. Maybe we could all become better.

Melampus We can practise by the beach. The show must remain ongoing no matter the situation.

That's not right, is it?

They exit. The lights dim and through the following transition we find some of the cast ruminating on some of **Thespis**' *ideas, as if doing their homework before the next rehearsal.*

The following overlap each other.

Atlas
THINK LIKE YOUR NEIGHBOUR.

Poly
DO AS YOUR NEIGHBOUR DOES.

Atlas
NOTICE HOW THEY BEHAVE.

Poly
HOW DOES IT FEEL?

Atlas
NOTICE YOUR NEIGHBOUR.

Poly
LIVE AS YOUR NEIGHBOUR LIVES.

Atlas
ARE THEY SCARED?

Poly
MAKE IT REAL.

Atlas
ARE THEY BRAVE?

Poly
MAKE IT REAL . . .

Atlas
BE BRAVE!

Poly
THAT'S WHAT ACTING IS!

Atlas
THINK LIKE YOUR NEIGHBOUR; THAT'S WHAT ACTING IS!

Melampus, **Poly**, **Thespis**, **Atlas** *and* **Adonis** *enter.*

Thespis Morning, everyone.

Poly Go!

Everyone
THEY SAY WHEN YOU PASS
PAST THE PARTHENON
PART OF THE PARTHENON
PASSES YOU BY!

All Except Adonis & Melampus
PART OF THE PARTHENON PASSES YOU BY . . .

Adonis, Melampus
PA! PA!

All Except Adonis & Melampus
PART OF THE PARTHENON PASSES YOU BY

Adonis, Melampus
PA! PA!

All Except Adonis & Melampus
PART OF THE PARTHENON PASSES YOU BY!

Tenors/Baris
PART OF THE PATH . . .

Altos
OF THE PATH . . .

Sopranos
OF THE PATH!

Adonis Trust falls! Boshus!!!

Melampus *catches* **Adonis** *perfectly.*

Group One
LA, LA, LA, LA, LA, LA
LA, LA, LA, LA, LA, LA!

Group Two
PASS PASS PASS PASS
PASS PASS PASS PASS
PATH PATH PATH PATH
PATH

Everyone
THEY SAY WHEN YOU PASS
PAST THE PATH TO THE PARTHENON
PART OF THE PARTHENON PASSES YOU BY.
YEAH!

Poly
WE'VE HAD NO RAIN FOR THIRTY DAYS.
I SEE NO END IN SIGHT.

Atlas
WE KNEEL AND TO THE GODS GIVE PRAISE.

Adonis *enters.*

Adonis
I AM SO FULL OF FRIGHT.

A moment of real joy.

Poly
LOOK IT IS OUR LEADER.
EVACTUS IS HIS NAME.

Atlas
HE LOOKS SO TIRED AND HUNGRY.

Adonis
DIONYSUS IS TO BLAME.

Thespis
WE'VE PRAYED FOR WEEKS FOR WATER!

Poly
BUT NOT A DROP DOES FALL.

Adonis
OH GOD OF GRAPE AND VINO,
WHAT'S THE MEANING OF IT ALL.
OH GOD OF GRAPE AND VINO,
WHAT'S THE MEANING OF IT ALL.

Everyone is shocked. They clap and cheer enthusiastically. **Adonis** *jumps for joy.*

Atlas Adonis that was fantastic.

Adonis Thanks, Atlas.

Thespis You've improved so much.

Adonis I had a little help from a great teacher.

Melampus *smiles.*

We jump forward again. The **Tyrant** *is in the amphitheatre with two builders (***Bard** *and* **Rhapsodes***).*

Tyrant The Dionysia tomorrow. I need you to increase the size of the amphitheatre!

Builder Two Have you planning permission?

Tyrant I don't need planning permission. I'm the almighty tyrant of Greece. I do whatever I want.

Builder One (*chuckling*) Good luck telling that to the council.

Builder Two And when do you want this done by?

Tyrant The morning!

Builder One Whoa! Steady on.

Builder Two Yeah, I mean Rome wasn't built in a day.

Builder One It's not been built at all yet.

Atlas *chases* **Thespis.**

Atlas Thespis! I got everything on your list. The props, the costumes, everything.

He reveals a bag full of costumes and intricate props, etc.

Thespis Atlas, you're a wonder!

Atlas And I made this.

Melampus, **Poly** *and* **Adonis** *wheel on a long canvas with a beautiful painting of the Ikarian coast.*

Atlas I figured since our prayer ends with the gods we need to take our audience to the heavens.

Thespis When did you do this?

Atlas Through the night.

Thespis I didn't know you could paint.

Atlas (*delighted*) Neither did I.

Thespis I think we're ready!

Melampus It's up to the fates now! Next stop Athens!

Poly And who knows, Lampy, maybe you'll even find your soldier there!

Something clicks. **Melampus** *has a moment of realisation.*

Melampus Yes! Maybe this isn't just it.

Dramatic chord.

Maybe I could change!!

Another dramatic chord.

Maybe I could work on my pelvic floor!

(*Sings bombastically.*)
BECAUSE WHO I AM!
ISN'T WHO I COULD BE!

Turning triumphantly to **Poly**.

Melampus
DARLING YOU'VE LIT,
A FIRE IN ME!

AND WHATEVER BATTLES,
MAY LIE IN STORE . . .

I'M GOING TO
FIND MY HANDSOME SOLDIER,
I'LL FIND MY HANDSOME HERO!
I'LL HOLD MY HANDSOME HERO!
ONCE MORE!

Fanfare. The **Tyrant** *stands on a balcony in Athens.*

All
LONG LIVE THE TYRANT!
LONG LIVE THE TYRANT!

LONG LIVE
THE
TY-RANT!

Tyrant I declare the first annual prayer competition open. Prepare to Di-onysia!

The **Tyrant** *exits. Back to Ikaria.*

Poly
I WROTE THE SCRIPT!

Atlas
I MADE THE COSTUMES!

Adonis
I LEARNT MY LINES.

Melampus
I TOLD THEM WHERE TO STAND.

Adonis
LEARNED ALL MY LINES.

Poly
PAINTED TREES.

Melampus
I SET THE SHOW.

Atlas
FOUND ALL THE PROPS WE'LL USE.

Everyone
I ACT LIKE YOU.
YOU ACT LIKE ME!

Thespis That's what theatre is!

Music builds and everyone sings different parts of the sequence over one another, the sound is swelling and growing.

Atlas
KNEEL TO THE GODS AND GIVE THEM PRAISE.
KNEEL TO THE GODS AND GIVE THEM PRAISE.

Poly
NOTICE YOUR NEIGHBOUR,
NOTICE HOW THEY BEHAVE.

Adonis
WHAT AN APPLE SEASON.
WHAT AN APPLE SEASON.

Melampus
LA, LA, LA, LA, LA,
LA, LA, LA, LA, LA, LA!

Thespis
PASS BY THE – PASS BY THE PATH
TO THE PARTHENON.
PASS BY THE – PASS BY THE PATH
TO THE PARTHENON.

Thespis *looks on, proud of what they have all created. Finally he signals for them to stop.*

Thespis Blackout!

Atlas What's that?

Thespis This!

Blackout.

V. The Dionysia

We're now in Athens at the first ever annual Dionysia. **Bard** *and* **Rhapsodes** *play lead singers for* **Rhodes**, **Crete**, **Naxos** *and* **Thebes** *plus the* **Host** *and* **Backing Singers**. *The rest of the cast multirole dancers and vocalists to the different competition entries.*

THE DIONYSIA

Loud 80s synth. SFX of cheesy **Hosts** *(played by* **Bard** *and* **Rhapsodes***).*

Backing Singers
IT'S THE FIRST DIONYSIA
YOU NEVER HEARD PRAYERS SPICIER

YOU NEVER SAW MERCH PRICIER
IT'S THE DIONYSIA!

IT'S THE FIRST DIONYSIA
THE STAKES COULDN'T BE DICIER
IF ALL GOES WELL,
WE'LL DO IT TWICE A YEAR
IT'S THE DIONYSIA!!

Bard Welcome Hades and gentlemen.

Rhapsodes To the inaugural Dionysia!

Bard The best prayer competition bar Parthe*non*. You do not want to Arte*mis* this!

Rim shot.

Rhapsodes Now it's time for our first competitor.

Bard The kids love them, the girls even more so.

Rhapsodes Give it up for Rhodes and the Bacchus Boys.

Pop-like music plays. **Rhodes** *(led by* **Bard***) performs a boy-band-style prayer.*

Bard

THERE ARE HUNDREDS OF GODS,
BOTH MIGHTY AND SMALL,
AND BABY YOU ARE MY FAVOURITE OF ALL.

YOU PICK UP THE TAB,
YOU COVER THE WINE!
AND FRANKLY BABY, THAT SUITS ME JUST FINE.

BUT SOMETHING SEEMS UP!
YOU USED TO BE COOL!
YOU USED TO HOST PARTIES AT YOUR POOL.
BUT HOW YOU'VE BEEN LATELY JUST SEEMS
CRUEL.

They dance in unison with matching hand gestures. They split into two groups. The lyrics overlapping neatly on the join.

Rhodes One
JUST GIVE US H2O –

Rhodes Backing
OH DIONYSUS!

Rhodes One
'CAUSE WE NEED IT HERE –

Rhodes Backing
HEAR OUR PRAYER.

Rhodes One
LET THE RAIN DESCEND

Rhodes Backing
SEND US WATER NOW

Rhodes One
LET IT NEVER END

Rhodes Backing
END THIS MADNESS NOW.

They come together again in perfect harmony, pointing at the audience, etc., as they swoon and scream.

Rhodes
ALL I WANT IS TO SPEAK WITH YOU,
'CAUSE DIONYSUS YOU'RE MY BOO.
IT'S SUCH A SIMPLE THING TO DO:
GIVE US RAIN!
PLEASE.

They strike a final pose to end their prayer. The hosts run forward.

Rhapsodes Wow! I've never Hera'd anything like it!

Rim shot.

Bard But now it's time for something a little sweet from the island of Crete!

Crete (*led by* **Rhapsodes**) *perform a crooner/dancer prayer.*

Crete Crooner
RAIN, WILL YOU TELL ME WHY YOU FLED?
WAS IT SOMETHING THAT I SAID?
THAT'S ALL I WANT TO KNOW!
RAIN

Crete Background
PITTA PATTER!

Crete Crooner
THE EARTH IS DRY AND FULL OF BLISTERS.

Crete Background
WOAH!

Crete Crooner
I'VE BEEN LIVING AT MY SISTER'S.
DID YOU REALLY HAVE TO GO.

THINGS WERE GREAT RAIN,
YOU FILLED MY CUP.
BUT SINCE YOU'VE BEEN GONE,
THINGS HAVE ALL DRIED UP:

THE DRAINS DON'T DRAIN.
THE FLOWERS WON'T FLOWER,
AND IT REEKS,
'CAUSE IT'S WEEKS,
SINCE I TOOK A SHOWER . . .

They shuffle/dance backwards. The **Host** *returns.*

Bard Amazing, amazing!

Rhapsodes You know tonight has been just like the eighth letter in the Greek alphabet.

Bard How you do mean?

Rhapsodes It's great Theta!

Bard And we're not Posei*don* yet.

Rim shot.

That's right, it's time for the moment we've all been waiting for. It's Thebes!

Clunk. Huge LX change. **Thebes** *(led by* **Bard***) perform an Ibiza dance prayer.*

Thebes One
OH DIONYSUS END OUR PAIN.

Thebes Two
PAIN. PAIN. PAIN. PAIN. PAIN.

Thebes One
END THIS CRISIS, SEND US, SEND US . . .

Thebes Two
SEND US. SEND US. SEND US.

Thebes One
RAIN. RAIN. RAIN.
RAIN.
RAIN. RAIN. RAIN.
RAIN.
RAIN. RAIN. RAIN.
RAIN.
RAIN. RAIN. RAIN.
RAIN!

Thebes Two
RAIN. RAIN. RAIN.
RAIN.
RAIN. RAIN. RAIN.
RAIN.
RAIN. RAIN. RAIN.
RAIN.
RAIN. RAIN. RAIN.
RAIN!

Thebes One
HEY BIG D YOU PUT THE WATER ON FURLOUGH.
SO WE CAN'T GROW THE GRAPES,
THAT MAKE UP THE MERLOT.

Thebes Two
AND IF WE CAN'T DRINK MERLOT,
WE CAN'T GET SLAUGHTERED,

Thebes One
AND FORGET THE FACT THAT WE DON'T HAVE
ANY WATER!
HEY WHAT HAPPENED?
WE TURNED OUR BACKS –

Thebes Two
AND SNAP!
– JUST LIKE THAT –
YOU TURNED OFF THE TAP!

Thebes One
SO A MESSAGE FROM THEBES,
ON BEHALF OF THE NATION:

Thebes Two	**Thebes One**
JUST GET OFF OF YOUR ASS, AND PRECIPITATE PRECIPITATION!	PRECIPITATION!

The **Host** *reappears, blown away.*

Rhapsodes That really was something.

Bard But like Diophantus the mathematician said to Homer. All these numbers are starting to Ili*ad* up.

Rim shot.

Rhapsodes So take a comfort break!

Bard Stretch your legs –

Rhapsodes And bend your arach*nes*.

Rim shot.

Bard We'll be right back with something we're hearing is a little bit different from the island of Ikaria.

Hosts wave. Music continues.

All So Far
IT'S THE FIRST DIONYSIA
THE STAKES COULDN'T BE DICIER
IF ALL GOES WELL
WE'LL DO IT TWICE A YEAR

IT'S THE DIONY-SI-A!

IT'S THE FIRST!
IT'S THE FIRST!
WE HAVEN'T DONE ONE BEFORE!

IT'S THE FIRST
DIO –
NY-SI
Y-SI
Y-SI
Y-SI
YS –

I –
A!!
GREECE!

VI. Behind the Scenes

We go 'backstage' at the Parthenon. The group are pacing nervously.

Poly How's everyone feeling?

Adonis Very good. I, Adonis the Grand Man of Ikaria, am ready and did not just sickus upus outside the Acropolis.

Melampus Hermes' Bow! Listen to the crowd out there.

Poly It's going to be okay.

Thespis Is it?

Athenian Soldier (*played by* **Rhapsodes**) *enters.*

Athenian Soldier This is your beginners' call, Ikaria. A reminder of our house rules. Your performance should last no longer than fifteen minutes, otherwise death. Do not make eye contact with the Tyrant, otherwise death, and if she sentences you to death no arguing, no crying, otherwise death by spike.

All (*with forced politeness*) Thank you.

Everyone smiles, thumbs up, etc. **Soldier** *exits and everyone drops the pretence.*

Adonis We must flee!

If we run now it will be okay. I have athlete's foot.

Poly How would that help?

Adonis It's a lucky charm.

He takes a severed foot from his satchel.

An old decrepit man sold it to me at the market. He said it belonged to an Olympian. As long as I have this with me I can outrun a horse.

Poly How did he get it?

Adonis What?

Poly How did the old man get the foot?

Adonis He said he chased down the Olympian and cut it off.

Melampus How would an old decrepit man run down an Olympian and cut off his foot?

Adonis You've got a good point. It would have been difficult. After all, the old man only had one foot.

Poly Can we please focus! We have to do this.

Melampus The show must insist upon itself regardless of emotional turbulence. No, that's not right either.

Thespis Pol, what if all this is a terrible idea?

Poly Thespis, listen. You've always said you were going to make it in Athens and I've always thought you were an idiot.

Thespis Great pep talk, Pol.

Poly And somehow, despite the odds, you have. Dad would be so proud.

Thespis You really think so?

Poly Did Selene the goddess of the moon really love Endymion?

Thespis Do you do it just to annoy me??

Poly I do . . . But Selene did. And Dad would be.

Thespis Thanks, Pol.

They hug.

Melampus Break a leg, everyone. Don't know why I said that.

Poly It's time . . .

<u>THE PERFORMANCE</u>

AND REMEMBER:
EVERYTHING'S GOING TO TURN OUT FINE.

Thespis
'CAUSE I'VE GOT YOUR BACK

Atlas
AND YOU'VE GOT MINE.

All
I ACT LIKE YOU
YOU ACT LIKE ME!

Poly *puts her hand in, followed by everyone else.*

VII. The Performance

They lift their hands. Music builds as the team run out onto the stage.

Poly
WE'VE HAD NO RAIN FOR THIRTY DAYS.

Melampus
I SEE NO END IN SIGHT.

Atlas
WE KNEEL AND TO THE GODS GIVE PRAISE.

Adonis *enters. Drum 'heartbeat' underscores. He is terrified.*

Adonis Oh no. I Errr . . .

Everyone suddenly fears for their lives.

Adonis (*with relief*) I AM SO FULL OF FRIGHT!

Melampus Oh, Dionysus! Why don't you hear us??

All
DIONYSUS! DIONYSUS!

Music shifts. **Thespis** *enters as Dionysus. He gives a fantastic performance.*

Thespis
I AM DIONYSUS,
GOD OF GRAPE AND WINE.

I HEAR YOUR ANGER,
I FEEL YOUR PAIN:
I DO, I DO.

AND YET YOU SPEAK OF ME SO POORLY,
KILL OTHERS IN MY NAME,
NOT KNOWING HOW IT FEELS
TO BEAR THE BURDEN OF YOUR BLAME.

I HEARD YOUR PAIN,
BUT MAYBE YOU FORGOT –
I CAN'T GRANT RAIN WHERE I AM NOT.

SO, PLEASE CONSIDER
IT MIGHT BE TRUE.
I'M JUST LIKE YOU.

JUST LIKE YOU.

The Tyrant Peisistratus *stands up.*

Tyrant
STOP IMMEDIATELY!

All The Tyrant!

Tyrant On your knees!

Everyone *drops to their knees. Tense percussion plays.*

Tyrant How dare you impersonate the gods? I demand to speak to the person responsible.

Beat.

Who is Thespis?

Tense music. **Melampus** *stands.*

Melampus I am.

Thespis What?

Melampus Everything you saw today is down to me.

Everyone is shocked. **Thespis** *stands.*

Thespis No. That's not right!

Melampus (*whispered to* **Thespis**) Not now.

(*To the* **Tyrant**) I am Thespis and if anyone must be punished it should be me.

Thespis No! I am Thespis. Punish me. This was all my idea.

Poly *stands.*

Poly No. I am Thespis. I wrote the script. I am responsible. Punish me.

Atlas *stands.*

Atlas Island rule forty-one. I am Thespis. Punish me.

Everyone looks at **Adonis** *who remains knelt on the floor.*

Adonis I think they should all be punished.

They all glare at him.

Adonis Fine. I am Thespis. Punish me.

Tyrant Guard, take them away. They will be put to death by Spike.

Guard *(played by* **Bard***) enters.*

Guard Come with me.

Tyrant Thank you, Spike.

Atlas *looks up to the heavens.*

Atlas Look!

ACT 1 FINALE

A shimmering, ethereal chord strikes up. Rain starts to fall.

Athenians (*softly*)
SHOWER US WITH RAIN

Atlas It's raining!

Melampus Gods be praised, the drought is over!

Athenians (*softly*)
SHOWER US WITH WATER

Poly Thespis, you've done it.

Thespis We've done it!

A pulse enters, as rain continues to pour. **Bard** *and* **Rhapsodes** *enter.* **Thespis** *turns to* **Poly**.

Thespis
YOU WROTE THE WORDS

And they were perfect!

Poly (*to* **Adonis**)
YOU LEARNT THE WORDS

All fifteen of them!

Adonis (*to* **Thespis** *and* **Atlas**)
YOU HAD THE IDEA!

Thespis/Atlas
WE DID!

Atlas *turns to* **Melampus**.

Atlas
YOU LED US THROUGH THE DROUGHT!

Melampus *smiles warmly.*

Melampus
AND MAYBE MY LOVE'S
JUST ROUND THE CORNER!

Athenians
AHHH
SHOWER US WITH RAIN!

Atlas
MAYBE HE'LL LOVE ME . . .

Poly
MAYBE I AM ENOUGH
MAYBE I AM ENOUGH!

Athenians
AHH
AHH

Adonis
I LEARNT MY LINES!

Poly
MAYBE I'M HAPPY!

Atlas
MAYBE I'LL SAY THOSE WORDS . . .

Melampus
MAYBE HE'S HERE

Thespis
MAYBE HE LOVES ME TOO . . .

All
I ACT LIKE YOU
YOU ACT LIKE ME!

Thespis
INTERVAL!

Bard What's that?

Rhapsodes It's this thing where the show stops and the theatre tries to sell you over-priced drinks and you spend most of the time in the queue to use the toilet.

Atlas That sounds awful.

Bard It is.

Blackout.

End Of Act One

Act Two

I. Entr'acte

ACT 2 OPENING

Lights up on **Thespis** *stood alone in a spotlight. Music is simple and gentle.*

Thespis

I AM DIONYSUS,
GOD OF GRAPE AND WINE.
I HEAR YOUR ANGER,
I FEEL YOUR PAIN.
I DO, I DO.

I AM DIONYSUS,
GOD OF GRAPE . . .

Lights up on vibrant Athens. Crowds gather around **Thespis** *as fans flock for his autograph.*

AND WINE!

Newsvendor *(played by* **Rhapsodes***) enters.*

Newsvendor Extra! Extra! Thespismania sweeps the capital!

Adoring Fans *scream as they spot him! 'It's Thespis!' 'OMZ! It's really him', etc.*

Thespis

I AM DIONYSUS,
GOD OF GRAPE AND WINE.

Fan *(played by* **Rhapsodes***) approaches.*

Adoring Fan Ahhhh!

Thespis *signs an autograph.*

Thespis
AND IF YOU THINK YOU'RE WORTHY,
COME AND WORSHIP AT MY SHRINE!

Fan *(played by* **Bard***) approaches.*

Adoring Fan I've seen you in everything you've done!

Thespis *signs an autograph.*

Thespis
I SEE MY PEOPLE'S PROBLEMS,
BUT THEY NEEDN'T FEAR BECAUSE,

Fan Three *with a baby (played by* **Rhapsodes***) approaches.*

Thespis
WELL, SOLVING PEOPLE'S PROBLEMS,
IS WHAT DIONYSUS DOES!

He kisses the baby.

Adoring Fan Three HE KISSED MY BABY!!

Thespis *poses with the* **Fans** *for a portrait.*

Thespis
SO CAST AWAY YOUR WORRIES,
TRUST IN ME AND YOU'LL BE FINE!
FOR I AM DIONYSUS . . .

Strikes a pose.

GOD OF GRAPE AND WINE!

*Greek Ern and Angela Athena (***Bard** *and* **Rhapsodes***) enter.*

Newsreader One I'm Angela Athena.

Newsreader Two And I'm Greek Ern.

Newsreader One It's been just over two months since Thespis and his fellow thespians took the world by storm and since then the rains keep falling.

Newsreader Two The crowds keep growing.

Newsreader One And Athens cannot get enough!

Newsreader Two And Athens cannot get enough!

We're outside the Parthenon. **Adoring Crowd** *(led by* **Bard** *and* **Rhapsodes***) wait in line at the box office.*

Adoring Crowd
THESPIS! THESPIS!
WE LOVE THESPIS.
AND HE LOVES US TOO.

We're with **Thespis** *at a promotional/ad event.*

Thespis I'm Thespis. I've walked in your sandals but now you can walk in mine! With new Thespis heeled wedges.

He holds sandals and smiles. We go back to the box office queue.

Adoring Crowd
IF YOU ASK US OUR HERO
– IF PUSH COMES TO SHOVE –
THERE'S ONLY ONE MAN,
THAT WE'RE DREAMING OF!

Thespis You'll sleep like a baby on the new Thespillow!

Adoring Crowd
NO, NO ONE IN ATHENS COULD RANK ABOVE,
THAT CHARMING, WITTY, SEXY, HANDSOME
THESPIS
WHO WE LOVE!

The **Crowd** *congas around the stage making their way to the theatre.* **Adonis** *joins in.*

Time jumps forward. **Thespis** *is spotted on the street.*

Fan One DO DIONYSUS!

Fan Two DO DIONYSUS!

Both Fans DO DIONYSUS!

Fan Three I'd do Dionysus!

Thespis Oh I really couldn't!

I AM DIONYSUS!
GOD OF GRAPE AND WINE!

Adoring Crowd
AHH! DO IT AGAIN PLEASE!

Thespis
I AM DIONYSUS
GOD OF GRAPE AND WINE!

Adoring Crowd
AH!
IT'S JUST SO GOOD!
MORE!

Thespis
I AM DI-O –

Adoring Crowd
YES! MORE!

Thespis
– NYSUS!

Adoring Crowd
MORE!

Thespis
GRAPE!

Adoring Crowd
PLEASE!

Thespis
GOD!

Adoring Crowd
MORE! MORE!

Thespis
GIVE ME A GOD!

Adoring Crowd
GOD!

Thespis
GIVE ME A GRAPE!

Adoring Crowd
GRAPE!

Thespis
GIVE ME A GOD, GRAPE!

Adoring Crowd
GOD, GRAPE!

Thespis
GIVE ME A:
GOD GRAPE, GOD GRAPE!

Overlapping voices.

Adoring Crowd
GOD GRAPE, GOD GRAPE
GOD GRAPE, GOD GRAPE,
GOD GRAPE, GOD GRAPE

Thespis
GOD GRAPE, GOD GRAPE
GOD GRAPE, GOD GRAPE,
GOD GRAPE, GOD GRAPE

Adoring Crowd Ahhhh!!!

Thespis
MY NAME IS . . .

Spotlight.

THESPIS,
I AM A LEGEND.
I KNOW IT SOUNDS A TAD IMMODEST . . . BUT IT'S TRUE.
BUT I'M ONLY STANDING HERE BECAUSE
OF FANS LIKE YOU!

Adoring Fan Zeus he means us!

Thespis
WELL I THINK YOU'RE A BUNCH OF LEGENDS
TOO!
YES I DO!

The **Adoring Crowd** *cheers and exits. We go the palace. The* **Tyrant** *is wheeled on in her golden bath.*

Tyrant What time will our guests be arriving this evening?

Advisor One I'm afraid we've just had word from the Pharaoh. He sends his apologies.

Advisor Two As does Cyrus the Great. He sends great, great apologies!

Advisor One Croesus king of Persia says something's come up.

Tyrant What's come up? Where the Furies is everyone?

Advisors *both look away, etc.*

Tyrant At least I'll have time to go over my acceptance speech for the gala tomorrow.

Advisor One About that . . .

Tyrant But I win most influential Grecian every year.

Advisor Two Maybe not this year . . .

Tyrant Then who? Why is this happening? We need to do something! I've got it!

WE'LL HOLD ANOTHER COMPETITION.
BETWEEN EACH COMMUNITY.

Advisor One Yeah . . .

Tyrant
WE'LL HOLD IT HERE ON TUESDAY

Advisor One Right . . .

Tyrant

IF THE AMPHITHEATRE'S FREE . . .

Music stops abruptly.

Advisor Two Which it isn't.

Tyrant Why?

Advisor One Well, Thespis is putting on his show.

Tyrant What, even Tuesdays?

Fine. We'll cancel it.

We'll just kill him.

Advisor One Well if you do that there might be a revolt on your hands. He's very popular, you know. You want to be careful.

Advisor Two Yeah people are really into that guy. He's got merch.

Tyrant Merch?

Advisor Two Yeah like, key-rings, goblets and robes, etc.

Advisor One It's actually quite good-quality stuff.

Opens jacket to reveal he's wearing a 'GOD OF GRAPE AND WINE' T-shirt.

Tyrant Fine. How about this.

WE'LL PUT ON OUR OWN PERFORMANCE.
INSTEAD OF THESPIS IT STARS ME!
WE'LL HOLD IT HERE ON THURSDAY
IF THE AMPITHEATRE'S . . .

It's not free is it?

Advisors/Yes Men No. No. It's not.

Advisor One They even do afternoon performances. It's mainly attended by older people.

Tyrant I think it's time we invited Mr Thespis over for some career advice. Send a messenger.

HE THINKS HE'LL WIN
BUT I WON'T LET HIM.
THIS MADNESS HAS TO STOP!

AND COME THE DAY I GET HIM,
I'LL BE BACK ON TOP!!!

Bath is wheeled off and we're outside the stage door. **Thespis** *moves through a crowd.*

We jump in time. **Thespis, Atlas, Poly, Melampus** *and* **Adonis** *sit on a big red kline (a sofa) with the* **Chat Host** *(played by* **Rhapsodes***) sat opposite them.*

Chat Host Thespis, you and your team are the talk of the town. It kinda feels like you're more loved than Zeus himself. Hahaha.

Thespis Just don't let him hear you say that.

Crowd laugh.

Chat Host Hahaha.

Thespis If you're listening, Zeus, smite him! Not me!

Crowd laugh.

Zeus *(***Bard***) appears from above wearing a 'THESPIS' T-shirt and various bits of 'THESPIS' merch.*

Zeus Don't you worry! I'm a huge fan!

Chat Host Now I know it's cheeky but could you give us a little taster from the show?

Poly Oh, I don't know.

Atlas We like to keep things under wraps.

Melampus Yeah. We couldn't possibly . . . Hit it!

Rim shot. Music starts back up. Now with a jazz vibe.

Melampus
WE'VE HAD NO RAIN FOR THIRTY DAYS!

Poly
I SEE NO END IN SIGHT!

Atlas
WE KNEEL TO THE GODS AND GIVE THEM PRAISE!

Percussion. Focus on **Adonis** *who whips his robe off to reveal he is wearing a sparkly smaller robe underneath.*

Adonis
I AM SO FULL!
I AM SO FULL!
I AM SO FULL OF FRIGHT!!

Poly/Melampus/Atlas
WAIT!

Adonis/Atlas
WHERE'S DIONYSUS?

Chorus
AHHH!

Melampus
WHERE'S DIONYSUS?

Chorus
AHHH!

Poly
THERE'S DIONYSUS!

Thespis
BEHOLD!
I AM DIONYSUS . . .
GOD OF GRAPE
AND WINE!

All
WINE!!!

Blackout.

II. The High Life

Lights up on a fancy apartment in Athens. The space is incredibly opulent, a beautiful fresco on the wall (no doubt painted by **Atlas***), a large open window looking out onto the Acropolis with an intricately designed Kline, chairs and a table in the centre. Wild flowers, wine and food (including many bunches of grapes) are dotted generously around the space.*

Thespis, **Poly**, **Atlas**, **Adonis** *and* **Melampus** *all stand together, raising a glass to one another after another successful performance.*

Melampus Well done, everyone!

Thespis What a night!

Atlas How many were watching?

Poly Over five thousand.

Adonis It's all like a dream; but one where I wake up dry and unashamed.

Poly I thought you were fantastic this evening, Adonis. Almost believable as a person.

Adonis *blushes.*

Adonis That means a lot.

Atlas To Adonis!

They all raise their glasses again.

Adonis To you all!

Thespis I think that's the best performance I've ever given.

Poly (*jokingly*) Oh, Thespis you say that every night.

Thespis And every night I mean it. When I entered they couldn't get enough!

Atlas (*teasing*) Not through want of trying!

Thespis What do you mean?

Atlas I'm teasing.

Poly I think Atlas is referring to you adding an extra ten minutes to your final speachus.

Thespis They always shout for more so I gave them more.

Beat.

Poly What do you think we should do next?

Thespis How do you mean?

Poly Well we can't do this forever, can we? I thought I could write us something new.

Melampus Sounds dreamy, Pol.

Thespis Like what?

Poly I was thinking of a retelling of Persephone Queen of the Underworld?

Thespis And who would I play?

Poly I don't know.

Adonis I have always wanted to play Hades! I would make a tremendous Hades. Watch. *I am Hades*!

Beat.

Thespis Look gang, let's not get ahead of ourselves. People love what we're doing now. They love my Dionysus.

Adonis (*knowingly*) And someone loves my Evactus!

Thespis What do you mean?

Atlas This came for Adonis earlier.

Melampus Is that a letter from the palace!?

Atlas An invitation from the Tyrant.

Adonis Commending my performance and offering her friendship should I ever require it . . .

Thespis What, really!?

Poly Thespis, don't be rude. But also really?!

Thespis It'll be a mistake. Just throw it with my other invites and fan mail.

Adonis Of course.

He pockets the note.

Thespis Zeus! I feel like everything I touch turns to gold.

Poly Careful with that. There's a reason King Midas didn't have children.

Nobody laughs.

I'm lost on all of you.

Thespis I'm just saying if ain't broken! You've got to admit life's pretty good at the moment.

Atlas Yeah, as long as Melampus' predictions don't come true.

Thespis Let's not get into this again, everything's great!

Adonis There's plentiful success and no sign of an Athenian arrow.

Melampus (*sadly*) The future stretches far and long, Melampus sadly is never wrong.

A heaviness hangs in the air.

Poly Let's get some rest. It's a two-prayer day tomorrow.

Everyone slowly starts to finish up for the evening. **Melampus** *puts on a coat.*

Atlas Lampy, surely you're not going out again?

Melampus A local told me of a home for ex-soliders north of The Agora. I thought I'd pop over, just in case.

Goodnight, all.

She leaves and everyone else starts to go to bed.

All Night.

Thespis Goodnight everyone.

Atlas Oh, Thespis, I was wondering if I could talk to you before bed.

Thespis Of course.

Everyone exits and **Atlas** *and* **Thespis** *are left alone. For a moment they are almost awkward in each other's company.*

Atlas What a wild couple of months!

Thespis You're telling me. Between the interviews, weekends with local leaders and the parties I can't remember the last time it was just us.

Atlas Four and half weeks ago on a Tuesday.

Thespis . . . What is it you wanted to go over?

Atlas I just wanted to talk about props. Do you think we need more grapes?

Thespis . . . this room is full of grapes?

Atlas Of course. Silly meus.

They laugh awkwardly. Beat.

Thespis . . . Well . . . Goodnight.

Atlas Also . . .

Thespis Yes?

Atlas I feel like your costume is looking a little tired. I might just patch your shirt up before the morning.

Thespis Okay.

Thanks, shall I just –

Atlas I can leave if –

Thespis No it's okay. I can . . .

He takes his top off.

Atlas *(softly to himself)* OMZ.

Thespis *offers his shirt.* **Atlas** *walks towards him. They stand at look at one another. Gentle music starts.*

Thespis What?

Atlas Nothing it's just . . .

Messenger *(played by* **Rhapsodes***) enters.*

Messenger Thespis of Ikaria.

Thespis *(frustrated)* Yes.

Messenger The Tyrant requests an audience with you immediately.

Thespis I'm sorry, Atlas. At least we know who Adonis' invitation was for now.

Atlas I'll be waiting.

Thespis *grabs a new robe and leaves.* **Atlas** *is once again left alone holding* **Thespis'** *shirt.*

Gentle music plays again.

‘____’

Atlas
ANOTHER CHANCE,
YOU'VE THROWN AWAY
WHY CAN YOU NEVER SEEM TO SAY
. . . ‘_’

He struggles, and fails, to say 'I love you' – nothing comes out. The notes to the words are played in the orchestra instead.

WHY IS IT
EVERY TIME YOU TRY
YOUR LEGS GO WEAK,

YOUR MOUTH GOES DRY
‘_’

WHY IS IT
EVERY TIME HE’S NEAR,
YOU FEEL YOUR COURAGE DISAPPEAR.
SO HE NEVER GETS TO HEAR
. . . ‘_’

AND WHAT IF?
WHAT IF YOU SAID?
THE WORDS YOU ALWAYS MEAN INSTEAD.
THE ONES YOU’RE SHOUTING IN YOUR HEAD . . .

HE MIGHT TURN HIS BACK ON YOU
PITY YOU
LAUGH AT YOU

IF ONLY YOU WERE SMART, AS POLY
OR CERTAIN, AS ADONIS.

IF ONLY YOU WERE WISE LIKE MELAMPUS,
OR MIGHTY LIKE THE TYRANT

IF ONLY YOU WERE SOMEONE ELSE
SOMEONE ELSE . . .

Wait a minute . . .

WHEN *YOU* TRY TO SAY THOSE WORDS
YOU MIGHT FILL WITH DREAD

BUT WHAT IF YOU ACTED,
LIKE A CHARACTER,
WHO SAYS THE WORDS INSTEAD?

YOU COULD PLAY THE PART OF SOMEONE
COURAGEOUS AND BRAVE!

WHO, FACED WITH ANY CHALLENGES,
WOULD KNOW JUST HOW TO BEHAVE.

AND WHEN YOU CAN’T SAY ‘THAT WORD’
IN FRONT OF ‘THAT MAN’ –

YOU JUST SWAP
YOUR SANDALS
WITH SOMEONE
WHO CAN!!

THEN, WHEN YOU SEE YOUR LOVE IS NEAR,
YOUR LEGS ARE FIRM YOUR VOICE IS CLEAR:

I LOVE YOU!

AND THINK, THE JOY THAT YOU WOULD FEEL
TO SAY THE WORDS, TO HIM, FOR REAL!
TO NEVER ONCE AGAIN CONCEAL:
I LOVE YOU!

AND THEN, AT LAST, THE WORLD WOULD SEE,
THE MAN YOU ALWAYS DREAMED YOU'D BE
SELF-ASSURED, AND STRONG AND FREE . . .

AND PERHAPS, ONE DAY,
YOU'LL COME TO VIEW
THIS VERSION OF YOURSELF,
AND YOU

AND FIND THE DIFFERENCES
WILL SEEM SO SMALL
YOU'RE NOT SO DIFFERENT
AFTER ALL . . .

BUT, FIRST, BEFORE THE WEEK IS THROUGH
YOU KNOW THE THING YOU HAVE TO DO . . .

YES, NEXT WHEN YOU SEE THESPIS
– DARLING, LOVELY, THESPIS –
YOU'LL SAY 'HOW'S YOUR DAY?'
AND 'BY THE WAY . . .'

I
LOVE
YOU.

He smiles warmly as the lights fade.

III. Looking For Love

The streets of Athens late at night. **Melampus** *enters. Mist drifts across the space.*

A low, thrumming tango beat begins to play.

<u>OLD MAN TANGO</u>

Melampus
EVERY NIGHT I GO OUT
TO SEE WHAT I CAN SEE
I HAVE MY CHAIN
I HAVE MY HEART
WHERE COULD MY LOVER BE?
AND SO, TO THE STREETS I GO,
TO DANCE:
THE OLD MAN TANGO!

A long line of old men appears and she goes down the line.

I SEE THESE MEN
I STOP AND SKIM
SO AS TO SEE IF
ONE IS HIM!

I SEE THESE MEN
I SEE THESE GUYS
BUT DO I SEE
MY SOLDIER'S EYES?

THIS ONE HERE
HE HAS NO TEETH
THAT'S NOT MY LOVE . . .

Keith (*played by* **Bard**)
MY NAME IS KEITH.

Old Men
HIS NAME IS KEITH!

Melampus
OR IS IT HIM;
IS HE MY TIPPLE?

NO, IT'S NOT HIM
HE HAS ONE NIPPLE.

Old Men
HE HAS ONE NIPPLE!

Melampus
THE OLD MAN TANGO!

Old Men
AH!

Melampus
THE OLD MAN TANGO!

Old Men
AH!

Melampus
WHERE DID MY MAN GO?
I MUST DANCE
THE OLD MAN TANGO!

COULD IT BE HIM?
RIGHT OVER THERE . . .
HE'S NOT MY LOVE

Man reveals hairy chest.

TOO MUCH HAIR . . .
THIS ONE'S TOO OLD
THIS ONE'S TOO YOUNG
THIS ONE'S NOT HIM
HE'S TOO WELL HUNG.

Old Men
HE'S TOO WELL HUNG!
WELL HUNG . . .

Melampus
THIS ONE'S TOO BORING
TOO DEBONAIRE
THIS ONE'S A WOMAN!

Claire (*played by* **Rhapsodes**)
MY NAME IS CLAIRE.

Old Men
HER NAME IS CLAIRE!
HER NAME IS CLAIRE.
CLAIRE!

Melampus
THE OLD MAN TANGO
THE OLD MAN TANGO.
WHERE DID MY MAN GO?

An **Old Man** *reveals and offers her a mango.*

Melampus
NO I SAID 'MAN GO!'
I MUST DANCE:
THE OLD MAN TANGO!

Dance, my old men! Dance for me!

Elaborate dance break.

EVERY DAY I WORK MY WAY THROUGH
HUNDREDS OF GERIATRIC MEN!
PRAYING ONE DAY SOON
I'LL HOLD MY SOLDIER ONCE AGAIN!
THIS ONE'S A TEACHER
NO! THIS ONE'S A COOK
NO! THIS ONE'S A PREACHER
NO! THIS ONE'S A COOK!

Stands next to very old-looking man.

THIS MAN IS THIRTY
OR SO HE SAID . . .
THIS MAN IS FLIRTY

A very old man (played by **Bard***) walks off very slowly (using a zimmer frame) in silence.*

THIS MAN HAS FLED.

Suddenly slower and sentimental, having spotted someone.

IS THIS THE MAN?
I SHOULD HAVE WED?
COULD IT BE HIM?

Old Men
NO! THIS MAN IS ALREADY DEAD!

They carry him off in a funeral procession.

Melampus
EVERY NIGHT IS JUST THE SAME
AN EXTENSION OF MY PAIN . . .
SO ON AND ON I GO:
SEARCHING, DANCING
THE OLD
MAN
TANGO!

IV. Drinks with the Tyrant

Music plays as we arrive at the Palace of **The Tyrant**. *A huge lobby with velvet drapes and golden furniture.*

Tyrant There he is!

Thespis (*bowing slightly*) Tyrant Peisistratus.

Tyrant Please, that was my father. Just call me TP.

It's an honour to have you in my home. My nephew's a big fan, he'd kill me if I didn't ask you to sign something for him.

Thespis Of course.

Tyrant Spike!

Spike *rips his shirt open and offers a knife. His torso reads 'cling onto power!'*

Tyrant Of course, you could just sign this instead.

Takes out legal scroll.

Thespis What's that?

Tyrant A contract. I want to build you your own theatre, a residency here in the capital.

Thespis That's incredible! I can't believe it. Pol's going to flip! I can't wait to see Atlas' face.

Tyrant Not so fast twinkle twinkle. This is a contract for . . . a one-man show.

Thespis A what?

Tyrant Oh, everyone's going to love them. You see, Thezzi, people like us are special. You're on the precipice of having everything you've ever wanted and there's only one thing you have to do to get it.

Thespis (*unsurely*) What's that?

Tyrant Take it.

Music starts

THE TYRANT'S SONG.

THE TIP OF MOUNT OLYMPUS
CAN BE A LONELY PLACE,
BUT DON'T YOU WORRY
DON'T YOU FRET.
I'M A FRIENDLY FACE

HERE TO OFFER GUIDANCE
TO GENTLY HOLD YOUR HAND
AND WALK YOU THROUGH
THE BITS OF FAME
YOU'RE YET TO UNDERSTAND.

THE PUBLIC REALLY LOVE YOU,
WELL THEY CLAIM TO LOVE YOU NOW,
BUT WHEN THEY ALL GET BORED OF YOU.
YOU'LL HAVE TO ACT.

Thespis But how?

Tyrant

CUT OFF YOUR FRIENDS!
DITCH THE LOT.
IF YOU WANNA STAY IN VOGUE.
DROP 'EM LIKE THEY'RE HOT.

CUT OFF THOSE LOSERS
LET 'EM ROT!
YOU OUGHT TO GET RID OF THEM,
THERE ON THE SPOT!

YOU THINK THAT FRIENDS CAN BE TRUSTED?
HA!
YOU THINK THAT FRIENDS ARE TO STAY?

Thespis But I love them!

Tyrant

YOU LOVE YOUR FRIENDS!?
I'M DISGUSTED
AT YOUR NAIVETÉ!

WELL SOON YOU'RE GUNNA SEE,
NOT EVERYONE'S AN HONEST GAL LIKE ME!

Thespis But I can't just cut them off? We've done everything together.

Tyrant Not what I've heard. My soliders said that back in Ikaria they tried to kick you out of the group . . .

Thespis Yeah . . . but things are different now.

Tyrant Hmm . . . STORY TIME!!

WHEN I WAS A TINY TYRANT.
I HAD A TINY FRIEND.
HE TRIED TO STEAL MY CROWN.

SO I KILLED HIM.

Thespis What?

Tyrant
WHEN I WAS A TEENAGE TYRANT
MY CLASSMATES GOT ON WELL
THEN ONE DAY THEY ALL LAUGHED AT ME.

Thespis So you killed them.

Tyrant Yes, I killed them.

THEN ONE NIGHT SOMETIME LATER,
MY MUM SENT ME TO BED
I DISAGREED PROFUSELY
YOU KNOW WHAT I DID?

Thespis Cut off her head?

Tyrant What?! No! What's wrong with you? This is my mother we're talking about!?

Thespis I'm so sorry.

Tyrant No, I'm joking, I killed her!

DESTROY YOUR FAMILY,
JUST ATTACK,
BETTER STAB 'EM IN THE FRONT
BEFORE THEY STAB YOU IN THE BACK.

YOU'RE THE WHEEL,
THEY'RE JUST GREASE
I'M JASON,
THEY'RE THE ARGONAUTS,
BUT YOU'RE THE GOLDEN FLEECE.

AS FOR YOUR TEAM,
I WOULD BE WARY,
OF DOUBLE CROSSING AND BETRAYAL.

Thespis Betrayal?

Tyrant
YOU'LL FIND THAT LOYALTY WILL VARY,
YOU'RE NOT TOO BIG TO FAIL.

BUT YOU DON'T NEED ANY OF THEM.
YOU ARE THE STAR!

Yes you are, darling!

YA DON'T NEED ANY OF THEM!

Hatcha!

YOU'RE BLOODY PERFECT,
JUST THE WAY YOU ARE!

Oh yes!

AND REMEMBER
I'M YOUR FRIEND.
AND I UNDERSTAND YOUR SITUATION!
LA-LA!

YOUR ONE TRUE FRIEND.
– THAT'S ME! –
WHO FORGOT TO TAKE HER MEDICATION.
LA-LA-LA . . .

Thespis This is mad. I can't do this to my friends.

Tyrant Why not? Don't you want to step out of your father's shadow? You could be bigger than yogurt.

Thespis It's all I've ever dreamed of!

Tyrant Darling boy, listen to your friendly Tyrant. Your pals are using you. As soon as another opportunity comes along they'll leave you behind. Don't you want to show the world what you can do!?

Thespis *looks crestfallen.*

Tyrant Oh, Poor Thezzi . . .

Remember Athenian Rule number one.

Thespis What's that?

Tyrant There are no rules!

YOU'RE BRILLIANT,
YOU'RE REFINED.
YOU'VE MORE TALENT IN YOUR FINGERS
THAN THE REST OF THEM COMBINED.

YOU'RE THE TALK OF THE TOWN!
YOU'RE WHERE IT'S AT!
YOU REALLY THINK THE OTHERS WON'T BE
JEALOUS OF THAT?

REALLLLY THESPIS?

SO DARLING BOY,
WHEN PERFORMING YOUR SHOW,
THE OTHERS,
HAVE TO,
GO!

CUT 'EM OFF!

Thespis I just don't know!

Tyrant Oh, baby . . . this is a big decision. If you have any questions you can get in touch. Here, take my number.

Gives **Thespis** *a piece of paper with a large number 1 on it.*

Tyrant YOU HAVE TWENTY-FOUR HOURS! Spike, take Thespis home in my personal chariot. He should get used to the trappings of success.

Thespis *is led away by* **Spike**.

Music.

Tyrant

AND SO THE PLOT WENT JUST AS PLANNED;
I'VE ONLY GONE AND GOT HIM
IN THE PALM OF MY HAND!
HA!

SO DARLING THESPIS
CAN NEVER GO WRONG –
BUT NOT FOR LONG!

Time for my bath – Hatcha!

V. The (Square) Wheels Come Off

Back in the apartment. **Melampus, Poly** *and* **Adonis** *are looking for* **Thespis.**

Melampus Any sign of him?

Poly Nothing.

Atlas *enters.*

Atlas I've looked all over town, nobody's seen him.

Poly We've got a performance in just over an hour, Atlas!

Adonis (*bravely*) I'll do it!

Melampus What?

Adonis I shall play the role like it's never been played before!

Poly I have no doubt of that.

Adonis Trust me! I know the lines. I've even made my own costume just in case. A hero is always prepared . . .

Melampus Is that why you asked to borrow my night linens?

Adonis It's just like Thespis' but with a little of my trademark flair.

Melampus Fine.

Adonis YES!! I shall not let you down!

He bows and runs off boyishly.

Poly Zeus! This isn't happening!!!

Atlas It's all my fault. I should have said something last night when he didn't come back.

Poly Don't worry, Atlas.

Melampus We've got a packed Parthenon this afternoon. Let's pray to Zeus he doesn't have to go on.

Thespis *enters.*

Thespis Who doesn't have to go on?

Poly Thespis! There you are.

Runs and throws her arms around him.

Atlas I'm just glad you're back. I have something to tell you.

Melampus Yes, Poly has big news. Go on!

Poly It's about my idea.

Thespis What idea?

Poly The one about Persephone? Remember!

Thespis Look, I can't see that working, Pol.

Melampus Well someone clearly does.

Poly I've had my first commission!

Atlas Congratulations!

Thespis What? Who from?

Poly It's a mystery. We found ten silver coins and a note at the door this morning.

Melampus It just said 'for Poly's next production.'

Atlas Fantastic! When do we rehearse?

Thespis Wait a minute, let's not spook the Trojan horses here. What about me as Dionysus?

Melampus This is a great opportunity for Poly.

Thespis Sure. I just think I need to decide if we're making big creative changes.

Melampus Well I'm our elder.

Atlas And director!

Thespis . . . Technically.

Melampus What's that supposed to mean?

Poly Let's talk about it later. How was the thing at the Temple.

Thespis What?

Melampus Oh, Thespis, you didn't forget did you?

Atlas He's under a lot of pressure at the moment. You know if you need, I can do some of the promotional stuff for you.

Poly Me too.

Thespis I can't believe I'm hearing this. I miss one event and you're all trying to replace me.

Melampus They're just trying to help.

Thespis It doesn't feel like that.

Poly Thespis what has gotten into you? Nobody's trying to replace you!

Adonis *enters wearing a bizarre makeshift outfit made from robes, bits from the apartment and fruits.*

Adonis

I AM DIONYSUS GOD OF GRAPE AND WINE AND I AM READY TO PERFORM!

Beat.

(*Insincere.*) Oh, yay, Thespis is back. I don't have to go on.

Thespis Zeus! I go away for one night and my role's being taken over by a fruit salad.

Poly (*amused*) No, you don't understand.

Thespis It's not funny, Pol. The talent is unhappy. I think we need a full company meeting.

Last night I had an offer –

Melampus – In great success there can be great unhappiness.

Thespis Not now, Melampus. We don't have time for your lady visions.

Atlas Thespis, why don't we chat when we're all back this evening. I really do have something I want to say.

Melampus I can't tonight. There's a veteran's event in the square and I –

Thespis Unbelievable! If you can see the future why can't you see the obvious. He's dead.

(*Under his breath.*) If he ever existed.

Poly Thespis! **Atlas** Thespis!

Thespis Why is it that everyone is more concerned about Melampus' made-up lover than the star of the show talking about something important?

Atlas He doesn't mean it, Lampy.

Thespis Don't tell me what I do and don't mean, Atlas.

Poly Thespis, you're being a jerk.

Thespis The Tyrant was right!

Poly Sorry, the Tyrant who threatened to kill us. You're listening to her now?

Thespis TP understands what it's like to be in my sandals.

Poly And tell me, what's that like? Because it looks pretty great to me.

Thespis You're just jealous because I stopped the drought.

Poly That was all you was it?

Atlas Come on, everyone, Remember island rule number twelve –

Thespis Oh my Zeus! We're not on the island anymore! Things are different now.

Atlas (*hurt*) You're right they are.

Poly It's okay, Atlas.

Thespis It's not okay. It's not okay that every step of the way you've all doubted me and now you're feeding off my yummy talent pie.

Melampus Once broken some things cannot be fixed –

Thespis Cram it, fortune cookie. I don't want your guidance.

Poly Then what do you want, Thespis?

Thespis . . . To show the world what I can do . . .

(*Takes out legal scroll.*) With this. A contract from the Tyrant to perform a *one man show.*

Poly I thought you'd grown up.

Remember what happened to Bellerophon after he killed the Chimera.

Thespis I don't know what happened, Pol, because I'm too busy creating an art form.

Poly Well maybe you should look it up.

Thespis Well maybe I will! And then I can be just like you and hide behind books whenever anything gets tough.

Adonis (*gentle*) Come on, Thespis. There's no need –

Thespis Back off, Adonis. I don't need life advice from a Pina Colada.

Adonis Hey, I'm your deputy Elder.

Thespis No you're not! You're not deputy Elder or head of the army, you're a joke. Do you know that everyone laughs at you? That nobody wants you around. Why I am even wasting my time with you all. I'm done.

Atlas Thespis please.

Thespis Do not follow me, Atlas.

Thespis *leaves. After a moment* **Atlas** *runs to his room, devastated. Heavy silence.*

Adonis Would anyone like a slice of pineapple?

Melampus I'll go and get him.

(*Calling after him.*) Atlas!

She exits.

Adonis You know in the military we always say . . . er . . . well we say . . . er well . . .

Poly Sorry, Adonis, not now.

She exits. **Adonis** *is left alone to reflect.*

VI. Wicked Betrayal

Music starts.

DOUBLE-DOWN

Adonis

CAN IT REALLY BE TRUE?
IS THIS HOW YOU'RE SEEN?
DO THEY LAUGH AT YOU IN PRIVATE,
HOW NAIVE HAVE YOU BEEN?

ARE YOU REALLY INEPT?
SHOULD YOUR BRAND BE REVISED?
IS IT TIME TO ACCEPT ADONIS,
THAT THE LOINCLOTH STUFFING'S . . .
ILL ADVISED.

IS IT TIME TO FACE THE FACT,
THAT THEY ALL JUST SEE THROUGH THE ACT,
IS IT TIME AT LAST TO,
STOP THIS STUPID SHOW?

DROP THE MASK,
AND LET GO?

NO.

I AM ADONIS.
I AM A LEGEND.
AND I WILL DO WHAT LEGENDS DO
AND DOUBLE DOWN.

I AM ADONIS,
I AM A HERO.
AND AS HEROES ALWAYS DO I'LL DOUBLE DOWN!

DID ICARUS REFUSE TO FLY WHEN THINGS GOT A LITTLE HOT?
DID PANDORA EVER STOP AND CRY OR DID SHE OPEN UP THAT BOX?
DID PROMETHEUS RUN FOR COVER?
DID MIDAS CONSULT A GLOVER?
DID OEDIPUS HAVE DOUBTS?
OR DID HE CRACK ON AND SCREW HIS MOTHER.

Backing singers appear behind him and the music swells.

All
HE SCREWED HIS MOTHER!

Adonis
AND WHEN FACED WITH HIS REFLECTION,
WAS NARCISSUS SCARED TO DROWN?
NO HE SCREAMED 'I AM PERFECTION,'
DUNKED HIS HEAD AND DOUBLED DOWN!

All
HE DOUBLED DOWN!

Adonis
DOUBLE DOWN.

All
HE DOUBLED DOWN, YEAH!

Adonis
I AM ADONIS.

All
HE IS ADONIS.

Adonis
I AM A HERO.

All
HE'S A HERO!

Adonis
AND I WILL DEMONSTRATE MY WORTH
SOMEHOW!

All
HE WILL SOMEHOW!

Adonis
I'LL MAKE THEM SEE THE BEST IN ME SOMEHOW!

All
WHAT A LEGEND! OOO! WHAT A LEGEND!

Adonis
SOMEHOW!

He takes out his invitation to the palace. Music darkens, danger and foreboding hang in the air.

Hello? (*echo*)

He's now stood in front of **Tyrant**.

Tyrant I was wondering when you were going to arrive.

Adonis (*bows*) I'm sorry to disturb.

Tyrant I always have time for a distinguished solider. How can I can help, darling?

Adonis *blushes.*

Adonis It's Thespis, he's ruining everything.

Tyrant I told him not to go it alone but he wouldn't listen!

Adonis He's upset everyone and he belittles me! He needs to be punished!

Tyrant Then let's do it together. Guards, take us to the Parthenon. Adonis has a big role to play tonight.

Music builds. We see **Thespis** *and* **Poly** *walking separately through the streets of Athens.*

Thespis
I AM AN ACTOR!

Adonis
I AM ADONIS!

Poly
I DON'T KNOW HOW THIS STORY ENDS . . .

Thespis
AND THEY DON'T NEED TO PLAY THOSE PARTS
I'LL DOUBLE UP!

Adonis
I'LL DOUBLE DOWN!

Poly
I THOUGHT WE WERE TOGETHER,
I THOUGHT THAT WE HAD GROWN,

Melampus
I SAW ALL THIS WOULD HAPPEN,
HOW COULD I ALLOW IT?

Poly
BUT NOW I SEE WE'RE OUR PATHS
SEPARATE AND ALONE?

Melampus
WHY DID I ALLOW IT?

Poly
I SHOULD'VE KNOWN TO DOUBT HIM,
BUT WE MUST CARRY ON WITHOUT HIM!

WE MUST WRITE ANOTHER STORY
ON OUR OWN . . .

Melampus
I MUST CALL OFF
THE OLD MAN TANGO!

Atlas *enters.*

Thespis
SO BY THIS TIME TOMORROW,
I'LL LEAVE THOSE AMATEURS BEHIND!

Atlas
OH THESPIS!

Thespis
I'LL STEAL THE SHOW,
AND THEN THE WORLD WILL SEE.

Atlas
HOW CLOSE I CAME, TONIGHT,
TO FINALLY REVEALING,
THIS FIRE THAT I'M FEELING.

Thespis
I WON'T NEED THE OTHERS THERE,
I'LL JUST BE ME!

Atlas
HOW WE WERE ALWAYS MEANT TO BE

Poly
I'LL NEVER SPEAK TO HIM AGAIN:

Thespis
I WILL BE:

Adonis
I'LL BE THE ONE TO BRING HIM DOWN:

Atlas
I LOVE YOU, THESPIS!

Thespis
THESPIS!

Poly
THESPIS!

Adonis
THESPIS!

All
THESPIS!

Thespis Give this contract to the Tyrant!

Spike *takes contract and exits.* **Adonis** *rushes forward and takes charge.*

Adonis
SO AS THE LEGENDS WHO CAME BEFORE ME.
I WON'T HIDE AWAY OR FROWN,
FOR THE WORLD WILL ALL ADORE ME;
THAT MAN OF GREAT RENOWN!
I AM A LEGEND,
AND LIKE A LEGEND,
I'LL DOUBLE DOWN.

All
HE'LL DOUBLE DOWN!

VII. A One-man Show

We cut to **Thespis** *backstage. A heartbeat-like percussion underscores as he paces around nervously before his big performance.*

<u>**THESPIS PERFORMS**</u>

Thespis (*muttering*)
THEY SAY WHEN YOU PASS
PAST THE PATH TO THE PARTHENON . . .

PART OF THE PARTHENON
PASSES YOU BY . . .

Spoken in time with the pulse underneath.

Arrows. Check.

Robes. Check.

Makeup. Check.

CALM THESPIS,
KEEP IT CALM.
YOU'VE GOT THIS.
YOU'VE GOT THIS.

Grapes.

Cloth.

CALM THESPIS,
KEEP IT CALM.
YOU'VE GOT THIS.
YOU'VE GOT THIS.

Looks in the mirror.

AND REMEMBER:
YOU WON THE PART.
YOU DESERVE TO BE HERE . . .

YOU DID CAST YOURSELF,
BUT STILL IT'S TRUE.
JUST BE YOU.

YOU'VE GOT THIS.
YOU'VE GOT THIS.
HAVE YOU GOT THIS?
HAVE YOU REALLY THOUGHT THIS THROUGH . . .
ARE YOU REALLY SO SURE
IT'S THE RIGHT THING TO –

Athenian Soldier *(***Rhapsodes***) enters*

Athenian Soldier Thespis.

Music builds and we follow **Thespis** *to centre stage. He's wearing the ancient Greek equivalent of a roll-neck jumper. He starts to play all the roles, clumsily changing hats etc as he goes. It's not great. The audience (***Bard** *and* **Rhapsodes***) interject.*

Thespis
WE'VE HAD NO RAIN FOR THIRTY DAYS.
I SEE NO END IN SIGHT.
WE KNEEL TO THE GODS AND GIVE PRAISE.
FRIGHT IS INSIDE OF ME!

No. Sorry.

Audience Member (*off*) What's he doing?

Audience Member Two (*off*) Do Dionysus!

Thespis *ignores and tries to continue.*

Thespis
LOOK IT IS OUR LEADER.
EVACTUS IS HIS NAME.

Audience Member (*off*) What's he doing?

Audience Member Two (*off*) Do Dionysus!

Thespis
HE LOOKS SO TIRED AND HUNGRY.

Audience Member Three (*off*) Where's all the cast?

Thespis It's a one-man show!

Audience Member (*off*) Sounds dreadful.

Audience Member Three (*off*) I want Poly!

Audience Member (*off*) Where's Melampus?!

Audience Member Two (*off*) Do Dionysus!

Thespis You do Dionysus!

The audience mumble in discontent, etc.

Thespis

WE'VE PRAYED FOR WEEKS FOR WATER!
BUT NOT A DROP DOES FALL.
OH GOD OF GRAPE AND VINO . . .

All Audience Do Dionysus!

Thespis I'm about to! Idiots!

All Audience Booo!

Suddenly the **Tyrant** *stands up in the crowd.*

Tyrant ENOUGH! The great people of Athens deserve more.

Thespis What?

Tyrant Citizens of Greece, Thespis isn't who you think he is! He's a talentless fraud. He cold-heartedly cut out his fellow friends, depriving you all because he couldn't bear to share the limelight –

Thespis No, you said –

Tyrant And don't just take my word for it. Listen to the newly appointed first ever head theatre critic from the *Daily Chariot* to confirm.

Adonis *walks onto the stage. He wears spectacles, a battered jacket and a pen behind his ear.*

Thespis Adonis?

Thespis *and the* **Tyrant** *look to* **Adonis**.

Tyrant What do you say?

Adonis (*unsurely*) Blasphemy! One star!

Thespis NOOO!

Adonis Thespis must be punished!

Tyrant Yes!

Adonis Ha. You're going to have your part taken away! How do you like me now?!

Tyrant Take him to the Mill House. Move with haste. He'll be put to death by Dawn.

Guard *(***Rhapsodes***) enters.*

Guard Come with me.

Tyrant Thank you, Dawn.

Adonis WHAT? BUT –

Tyrant Goodbye, Thespis.

Thespis *is led away as the crowd cheer, baying for blood.* **Adonis** *watches on horrified. He runs off.*

VIII. Returning Home

We arrive outside the apartment where **Poly** *and* **Atlas** *have packed all their belongings into a square-wheeled cart, ready to return to Ikaria.*

Poly There, done.

Atlas I'm going to miss this place.

Melampus *enters with her bags, etc.*

Melampus Right, that's the last of it. Time to go.

Atlas (*heartbroken*) Oh, Poly, do we really have to do this? What about your commission?

Poly I'm not interested.

Atlas But maybe Thespis will change his mind. You know what he's like, any minute now he'll burst in and –

Poly I'm done waiting for my brother to learn lessons that none us of have ever needed to learn. Let's just go home.

Melampus (*sadly*) There's nothing keeping us here.

Poly I'm sorry you didn't find your soldier, Melampus.

Music plays, wistfully.

Melampus
WELL, THAT'S JUST THE WAY LIFE GOES.
YOU CAN'T WISH AWAY YOUR WOES.
HE'S OUT OF MY LIFE . . .

I should've let him go the day the birds took him. It is what it is.

Atlas (*crushed*) Yeah.

Adonis *bursts in, alarmed and breathless.*

Adonis Melampus!

Poly Adonis.

Atlas What's wrong?

Adonis Okay. You have to promise to not be angry with me?

Poly Adonis, just spit it out!

Adonis *looks around unsurely.*

Adonis Fine. It's possible that in a bid to prove my worth I accepted the Tyrant's invitation, took a job at a state-run news outlet and framed Thespis for Blasphemy.

Poly/Atlas What!?

Melampus Where's Thespis now?

Adonis That's the bad bit. He performed his one-man show, I gave it one star, the audience turned and the Tyrant sentenced him to death.

Poly Adonis, how could you?

Adonis I was trying to help! I thought if I could teach Thespis a lesson then maybe everything would go back to how it was.

Poly By arranging to have him executed?!

Adonis I didn't think they'd kill him. I just thought they'd make him play sword carrier in the next production.

Poly You've betrayed all of us, Adonis.

Melampus Melampus is always –

Adonis Yeah, Yeah, Yeah! You're always right and I'm a disgrace and soon I'll be killed by an arrow!! I'm not Adonis the Grand Man of Ikaria. I'm a weak and small little man!

Atlas It's okay, Adonis –

Adonis I'm not even Ikarian. I'm from Crete.

Melampus What are you talking about, Adonis?!

Adonis And that's not my name!

Melampus What?

Adonis I just made it up. My real name is Andrew Gibbons!

Melampus Zeus' papoose!

Adonis I am Andrew Gibbons of Crete, I'm not a soldier, I'm a trained accountant who lives with his mother and I am very, very sorry!

Atlas Now let's all remember island rule number eighty-two!

Melampus Atlas, stop with the stupid rules! I made all one hundred and thirty-seven of them up so I could take your food rations and get you to trim my excess back hair.

Atlas (*appalled*) Rule number one hundred and twenty-nine. When the Lampy's back is thick and woolly make sure Atlas shaves it fully!

Adonis (*crying*) You're a terrible person.

Melampus You're one to talk!

Poly Wait. The handwriting on the note I received to commission a new play is the same as the handwriting on Adonis' invitation from the Tyrant.

Atlas What does that mean?

Poly It means the Tyrant has been trying to tear us apart all along.

Adonis So what do we do now?

Atlas Island rule eighty-two . . .

Melampus They're not real!

Atlas Well that might be the case but I've lived my whole life by those rules and they've made me a better man. They've reminded me that we're something bigger than our mistakes. Island rule eighty-two.

WHATEVER TROUBLES WE MAY FIND,
WE NEVER LEAVE A FRIEND BEHIND.

Melampus We have to save Thespis!

Adonis But how? We can't just walk into the Mill House, collect Thespis and walk out unchallenged?

Poly Or maybe we can?

<u>THE PLAN</u>

Music starts.

Melampus How do you mean?

Poly *We* can't but *the Tyrant* and her guards can. Atlas, do you think you could make a Athenian cape out of these drapes?

Atlas I could give it a go and if I need help there's a haberdashery across the road.

Rhapsodes *enters.*

Rhapsodes TOLD YA!

Rhapsodes *exits.*

Poly And, Melampus, did they have any spare helmets at the veterans' home?

Melampus Tonnes.

Poly We're going to use the very thing that got Thespis into the Mill House to get him out.

Atlas Adonis' fragile ego?

Poly Acting. Adonis and Melampus . . .

YOU PLAY THE GUARDS.

Adonis Will do, boss.

Poly
I'LL PLAY THE TYRANT.

Melampus Of course. That's brilliant!

Poly I'll say I've had a change of heart. We'll walk in, tell the guards their shift has ended, collect my brother and just walk out the door. And, Atlas –

YOU BE THE LOOKOUT.
SHOULD ANYTHING GO WRONG.
THEN YOU MUST WAIT NEARBY.

YOU'LL HAVE A GETAWAY VEHICLE
SO WE'LL MOVE QUICKER THAN THEY CAN.
DO YOU LIKE MY PLAN?

They cheer enthusiastically

Poly Of course you do!!

FOR WE ARE THE ISLE OF IKARIA,
THE NOBLEST ISLAND IN GREECE!

AND WE HAD THE GUTS
TO INVENT THE PLAY
THAT ENDED THE DROUGHT,
AND SAVED THE DAY

AND YES WE MIGHT,
BRIEFLY, HAVE
LOST OUR WAY

BUT NOW, WE'RE BACK!
BY ZEUS, WE'RE BACK!!

LET'S HEAR A CHEER
FOR IKARIA

They cheer!

Poly
OUR BEAUTIFUL PALACE
OF PEACE

Atlas
WHERE IF ONE FALLS,
WE'LL ALL COME RUNNING

Melampus
ARMED WITH
COURAGE,

Adonis
GRIT,

Atlas
AND CUNNING!

Melampus
WE'RE UNITED,
UNLIKE SOME!

Atlas
HOLD ON,
THESPIS,
HERE WE COME!

Poly
AND THOUGH
THAT TYRANT
DERIDES US,

AS SHE HIDES
IN HER DEN

WE BEAT THEM
BEFORE, AND WE'LL
BEAT THEM
AGAIN!

All Yeah!!

Poly
AND NOW I SEE QUITE CLEARLY
AS MY BACK'S AGAINST THE WALL . . .

THAT ALL MY LIFE I'VE DOUBT MYSELF
AND NEEDN'T HAVE AT ALL!

FOR STANDING HERE AND LEADING YOU
I'VE COME ALIVE AT LAST

LIKE THE IDOLS WHO HAD
SO IMPRESSED THE POLY OF THE PAST

AND ISN'T IT RATHER IRONIC?
THAT MY BROTHER IS STUCK IN A TIZ . . .

WHILE THE HESITANT GIRL FROM IKARIA
KNOWS EXACTLY
THE WOMAN
SHE IS!

They all cheer 'POLY!'

SO LONG LIVE
THE ISLE OF
IKARIA!

Adonis
MAY OUR FORTUNE
FOREVER INCREASE!

Atlas
SAFE, AND AT HOME
IN IKARIA.

Poly
THE HAPPIEST,
HEALTHIEST

Atlas
LIVELIEST,
LUCKIEST,

Melampus
SUNNIEST,

Adonis
STEALTHIEST,

Poly
GRITTIEST,

Melampus
PLUCKIEST,

All
NOBLEST
ISLAND IN –

They all take a big breath.

GREECE!!

Rousing play-off music builds as they march off into the distance to enact their plan.

IX. Just Thespis

Spotlight fades up. **Thespis** *is in the Mill House, shackled and chained to a small wooden bed (DSC). It's a stark space full of heavy bars, dingy lighting and thick pillars. He's watched by a very* **Old Guard** *(played by* **Bard***).*

WORLD OUT THERE REPRISE

Thespis
THERE'S A WORLD OUT THERE,

THERE'S A WORLD OUT THERE.
BEAUTIFUL, FRIENDLY AND FREE.

THERE'S A WORLD OUT THERE, NO –

THERE'S A HOME OUT THERE.
AND IT'S WHERE I WAS DESTINED TO BE!

THE NEVER-ENDING SUNSETS,
THE SALTY SEA-SIDE AIR.
IT WAS HEAVEN, AND YOU HAD IT,
YOU SHOULD'VE STAYED RIGHT THERE

BUT YOU HAD TO GO AND SEE THE WORLD,
SOMEHOW . . .
WELL YOU'VE SEEN IT NOW!

AND WHAT DID IT COST YOU?
ONLY YOUR LIFE.
ONLY THE PEOPLE YOU LOVE.

AND EVERYTHING YOU DREAMED WAS THERE.
ALL YOU EVER DREAMED WAS RIGHT THERE IN
FRONT OF YOU;
YOUR FAMILY, YOUR TRIBE –
THE FRIENDS WHO LOVE YOU . . .

Guard, do you know what happened to Bellerophon after he killed the Chimera?

Old Guard He thought he was a god, tried to climb Olympus and fell to his death.

Thespis Oh.

Old Guard Not long now . . . Dawn approaches.

Thespis Morning already?

Dawn Helllooo.

Old Guard Alright, Dawn.

X. The Plan in Action

Poly, **Melampus** *and* **Adonis** *arrive outside the Mill House.* **Poly** *is dressed as the* **Tyrant** *whilst* **Adonis** *and* **Melampus** *are guards. Their costumes aren't bad but they look a little homemade. Two real* **Mill House Guards** *(***Bard** *and* **Rhapsodes***) stand on the other side of the stage at a door. They both hold brown leather shields and large scythes and which they use to block the entrance/ exit.*

Suspenseful music.

Poly (*with urgency*) Okay everyone, remember, stick to the plan.

Adonis Wait, Poly, I've been thinking. Who am I?

Poly We've been over this. You're a guard.

Adonis But I mean, who is he? What makes him tickus?

Melampus Just work it out as you go along.

Poly And act natural and don't do anything that'll draw attention to us.

Adonis *and* **Melampus** *straighten their helmets, etc.* **Poly** *pulls a small veil across the top half of her face.*

Poly Come on.

Music shifts. They walk over to the real guards. **Poly** *(as the* **Tyrant***) clears her throat and acts with confidence.*

Mill House Guard One (*bowing slightly*) Your Excellence!

Mill House Guard Two We weren't expecting you?

Poly I need to see the prisoner, out of my way.

Mill House Guard Two Of course.

Melampus Good-day.

Both Guards Good-day.

Adonis (*very affected and unusual performance*) Good-dayy!

Mill House Guard One Who are you?

Adonis *is very nervous. He dries.*

Adonis I'm erm . . .

Unsure of what to say he points at things that he can see.

Scythe. Man. Robe. Sun. Brown.

Poly Simon Robson Brown!

Adonis Yes! I'm Si-mon Robson Brown and I'm working out who I am as I go along.

Mill House Guard Two Aren't we all, brother.

Poly Guards, you may leave. Simon Robson Brown and his colleague . . . Maximus Grippus will take over.

Guards Long live the Tyrant!

Adonis Long live the Tyrant!

Melampus Long live the Tyrant!

Adonis Long live the Tyrant!

The guards exit. Fanfare as **Poly**, **Adonis** *and* **Melampus** *enter the Mill House (from USC).* **Thespis** *remains shackled to the bed (DSC).*

Music shifts. Rhythmic and upbeat.

THE ESCAPE

Poly Where's the prisoner?

NOW LISTEN, GUARD,
A CHANGE OF PLAN!
GET THE KEY,
RELEASE THIS MAN!

Old Guard
OF COURSE, YOUR EXCELLENCE,
OF COURSE, OF COURSE, OF COURSE!

Old Guard *whistles jovially. He takes out a large set of keys and starts to unlock* **Thespis** *from his various chains.*

Poly
YOU'RE PARDONED NOW AND FREE TO GO!

Old Guard
YOU LUCKY LITTLE SO AND SO!

Melampus
LONG LIVE THE TYRANT! LONG LIVE THE TYRANT!

All
LONG LIVE THE TYRANT!

Fanfare as the real **Tyrant** *enters.*

Adonis The Tyrant!

Poly *spots the* **Tyrant** *and dives behind a pillar.* **Old Guard** *finishes unchaining* **Thespis**.

Old Guard
NOW OFF YOU GO, LIVE LIFE, HAVE FUN!

Tyrant
YOU FOOLISH GUARD WHAT HAVE YOU DONE?

Old Guard
I FREED THE PRISONER!

Tyrant
I DON'T UNDERSTAND?

Old Guard
BUT WHY?

Tyrant
YES WHY!

Old Guard
'TWAS YOUR COMMAND?

Tyrant
I SAID NO SUCH THING,
YOU STUPID MAN.
NOW CHAIN HIM UP
AS FAST YOU CAN!

Old Guard
OF COURSE, YOUR EXCELLENCE!
OF COURSE, OF COURSE, OF COURSE!

Music starts to speed up. The **Old Guard** *whistles a little quicker, as he begins to chain* **Thespis** *back up. The* **Tyrant** *looks at* **Adonis** *and* **Melampus** *and senses something is off.*

Tyrant And who are you?!

Adonis I'm Simon Robson Brown.

Melampus And I'm Maximus Grippus.

Tyrant I haven't seen you before?

Melampus . . . We're . . . locum workers . . .	**Adonis** . . . We're . . . locum workers . . .

Melampus *takes charge of the situation.*

Melampus
YOUR EXCELLENCE,
THANK ZEUS YOU'RE HERE.
FOR HALF THE
PERSIAN GUARD ARE NEAR.

WE HAVE TO FLEE,
BEFORE THEY FIGHT,
SO COME WITH ME,
CAUSE TIME IS TIGHT!

Tyrant
THAT CAN'T BE RIGHT,
I'VE BEEN OUTSIDE,
I SEE NO NEED,
TO RUN OR HIDE!

Melampus
BUT YOUR EXCELLENCE,
THEY'VE BREACHED THE TOWN . . .

Adonis
AND I AM SIMON ROBSON BROWN!

Melampus Come with me if you want to live!

She grabs the **Tyrant** *and drags her off (USC). Music speeds up a little more.* **Poly** *jumps out of hiding, making it appear as though she has magically appeared on the other side of the room. The* **Old Guard** *finishes re-applying* **Thespis'** *shackles.*

Old Guard
I'VE CHAINED THE PRISONER BACK TO THE BED!

Poly
BUT WHY?

Old Guard *(in rhythm)*
BECAUSE THAT'S WHAT YOU SAID?!

Poly *(in rhythm)*
YOU THINK THAT'S WHAT I SAID,
BUT NO!
UNCHAIN THIS MAN,
AND LET HIM GO!

Music speeds up.

Old Guard
OF COURSE YOUR EXCELLENCE,
OF COURSE, OF COURSE, OF COURSE!

Adonis
LONG LIVE THE TYRANT! LONG LIVE THE
TYRANT!

All
LONG LIVE THE TYRANT!

With the **Guard***'s focus on* **Thespis**, **Poly** *removes the little veil around her face.*

Poly
LOOK, DEAR BROTHER, CAN'T YOU SEE!

Thespis
OH ZEUS IT'S POLY!

Poly (*shushing him*)
YES IT'S ME.

Fanfare. The **Tyrant** *re-enters with* **Melampus** *chasing her.*

Poly
ZEUS!

Melampus
COME BACK!

Tyrant
BUT WHY?

Melampus
THAT DOOR IS BARRED.

Tyrant
AND YET!

Melampus
AND YET?

Tyrant
NO PERSIAN GUARD!

Poly *jumps behind the pillar.* **Old Guard** *has unshackled* **Thespis**.

Old Guard
BEFORE SHE U-TURNS,
RUN FROM HERE!

Tyrant
YOU FOOL! I'VE BEEN COMPLETELY CLEAR!
RESTRAIN THIS MAN AT ONCE!

Old Guard
OR WHAT?

Tyrant
I'LL EXECUTE YOU ON THE SPOT!

Old Guard (*getting frustrated*)
OF COURSE! YOUR EXCELLENCE!
OF COURSE! OF COURSE . . .

Old Guard *chains* **Thespis** *up again, whistling incredibly quickly as the music speeds up again.*

Adonis (*shouting in panic*)
YOUR EXCELLENCE!

Tyrant
NO NEED TO SHOUT!

Adonis
WE NEED TO TALK!

Tyrant
THEN SPIT IT OUT.

Adonis
IT'S PRIVATE PLEASE JUST COME THIS WAY.
WE MUST CONFER!

Tyrant
NO, LET'S DELAY!

He pulls at the **Tyrant**, *trying to get her to follow him.*

Adonis
IT'S URGENT THOUGH!?

Tyrant
BUT WHAT'S THE REASON!

A handful of apples fall from **Adonis'** *robes.*

Adonis
OH ZEUS IT MUST BE APPLE SEASON!

Please, your excellence, it will only take a moment.

He drags the **Tyrant** *out of the room.* **Poly** *pops up.*

Poly
REMOVE HIS SHACKLES ONCE AGAIN!

Old Guard
PLEASE, YOUR EXCELLENCE, PICK A LANE!

He unchains **Thespis**.

Melampus
LONG LIVE THE TYRANT.
LONG LIVE THE TYRANT.

All
LONG LIVE
THE
TY-RANT!

LONG LIVE
THE
TY-RANT!

The **Tyrant** *comes straight back in with* **Adonis** *chasing after.* **Poly** *jumps out of the way.*

Tyrant
NO MORE DEFERRAL,
ALL IS FINE.

Adonis
PLEASE JUST TAKE A LITTLE TIME!

Old Guard
UNCHAINED AND FREE.

Tyrant
YOU'RE KIDDING ME.
THIS GUARD IS SENILE,
DIM AND OLD!

Old Guard
ARGHHHH!

Tyrant
ARGHHHH!

Melampus
ARGHHHH!

He starts to chain **Thespis** *up again.* **Melampus** *has had enough and punches the* **Tyrant** *in the face, knocking her out.*

Melampus
THAT BUYS US TIME,
SHE'S OUT STONE COLD!

Adonis *and* **Melampus** *drag the* **Tyrant** *behind the pillar whilst the* **Old Guard** *continues to chain* **Thespis** *to the bed.* **Thespis** *looks on exasperated.*

All
LONG LIVE THE TYRANT!
LONG LIVE THE TYRANT!
LONG LIVE
THE TY . . .

Poly *jumps out but her costume gets caught on an ornate trim on the pillar. As she moves forward her costume, including her face covering, is pulled away and she is revealed.*

Poly
NOW LISTEN, GUARD, OR I'LL GET CRUDER –

Old Guard
WAIT A MINUTE!
HELP!
INTRUDER!

Atlas *enters.*

Atlas
THE TYRANT'S HERE! WE NEED TO DASH!

Guard
TRICKSTER YOU HAVE MET YOUR MATCH!

Atlas
WHAT'S GOING ON?

Thespis
IS THIS GOODBYE?

Old Guard
SORRY PAL, PREPARE TO DIE!

Huh, where are my keys?

The **Old Guard** *points his arrow at* **Poly**. **Adonis** *grabs the* **Old Guard***'s keys. He holds them aloft.*

Adonis
AH-A! A CUNNING INTERVENTION!
THE FINAL PART OF MY REDEMPTION!

Atlas
CAREFUL, ADONIS!

Adonis
MISSION COMPLETE!
AND THAT'S NOT MY NAME!

I'M ANDREW GIBBONS,
THE ACCOUNTANT!
FROM CRETE!!!

The action snaps into slow motion. **Old Guard** *aims his bow at* **Adonis**. *He shoots.* **Melampus** *runs forward and jumps in the way of the arrow.*

Old Guard (*firing*) Argh!

Melampus (*slow motion*) Noooo!

Poly/Atlas/Melampus (*slow motion*) NO! (*etc*)

Melampus *is hit. She falls to the ground.* **Adonis** *rushes to her and the music cuts out.*

Adonis No! Melampus!

He holds **Melampus** *in his arms.*

Adonis You knew that arrow was meant for me! I was supposed to die not you!

Melampus Perhaps . . . Melampus isn't always right after all.

Melampus *dies. Silence.*

Adonis Melampus . . . Melampus?

Beat.

She's gone.

Silence. Everyone is devastated.

Old Guard Melampus? . . . Not Melampus of Ikaria?

Poly The very same.

Old Guard Why I have spent my whole life searching for her. You see many years ago we were betrothed but on the day of the wedding I was heading to the temple and I was . . .

All Carried away by birds in the direction of the capital!

Old Guard How in the name of Zeus did you know?

Adonis She too spent her years in search of you.

Poly You were the love of her life.

Old Guard And she mine.

The loss suddenly hits him. It's unbearable.

Tragedy on top of misery! I cannot bear it! Argh!

He stabs himself.

I will find you in Hades, my Aphrodite.

Collapses and dies.

Thespis
WHAT IS HAPPENING!?!

Poly *unbinds* **Thespis**.

Thespis Pol! You came back for me?

Poly Did Orpheus come back for Eurydice in the underworld?

Thespis (*he knows this one*) He did! Oh Pol, I'm so sorry. How I treated all of you was unforgivable and now Melampus and that incredibly old guard are dead and it's all my fault. When we get home I'm going to spend every day making it up to you.

Adonis I'd give anything to be the one lying there instead of you, Melampus. You're gone, I betrayed my friend and nobody will ever want to have anything to do with Adonis the Grand Man of Ikaria again.

Poly No, maybe not. But I would like to get to know Andrew Gibbons a bit more. He seems like a nice man.

Adonis Oh, Poly thank you!

They hug.

Melampus *stirs.*

Melampus Ohh! Ohh!

Thespis Melampus! You're alive.

Poly How?

Melampus *reveals the locket she wears around her neck.*

Melampus The arrow hit the locket. My solider saved my life!

She takes the locket off. It's a moment of closure for her.

Atlas True love's gift shall save the day!

Adonis (*full of joy*) Melampus is always right!!!

Melampus Wherever he is he must still care about me.

Adonis (*moved to tears*) I know he does! And if he was here he would tell you that he never stopped loving you.

Melampus Do you think I'll find him?

Adonis I think it's highly unlikely.

Melampus Then maybe it's time for me to let him go.

She takes off her locket. **Adonis** *and* **Melampus** *hug.*

Thespis I think we all need to go, before it's too late.

Poly The Tyrant's sure to be back at any moment.

The **Tyrant** *steps out from behind a pillar.*

Tyrant Yes. She is . . .

All gasp, etc.

Tyrant I've had enough of all of you! I have been humiliated, dismissed and now I'm afraid it's time for you all to die! Guards!

More **Guards** *arrive.*

Atlas No wait! Just . . . just . . . Try to put yourself in our sandals!

Musical sting.

Tyrant What?

Gentle music spikes.

Poly We're from a tiny island across the sea.

Melampus And we were forced to come to Athens!

Thespis And we came up with a new kind of prayer.

Adonis And I've been living a lie all my life.

Melampus And I lost the love of my life.

Poly And we lost our father.

Thespis And I lost my way.

Adonis And I lost my temper and betrayed everyone.

Atlas And throughout all this I've never been able to tell Thespis that I love him.

Thespis And I've been too blinded by my ego to see that I love Atlas too.

Atlas You do?

Thespis Did Achilles love Patroclus?

Poly Nice

Atlas OMZ! And I found out Thespis loved me.

They embrace.

Melampus And we forgave Adonis.

Poly And came up with a plan.

Adonis And sacrificed ourselves.

Thespis And I was saved!

Poly And now we're here. Asking you to let us go home.

Beat. Suspense.

Tyrant (*struggling*) But I can't just let you go. You don't understand. Nobody understands!

Poly I think I do.

Music shifts.

MY NAME'S THE TYRANT.

Tyrant It's Michelle actually.

Poly
MY LIFE IS RUBBISH.

Tyrant How could you know?!?

Poly
YOU'D THINK MY LIFE'S SECURE AND SET,
AND YET IT'S RUBBISH.

THOUGH I MIGHT POSSESS A MIGHTY THRONE,
I SIT IN MY PALACE ALL ALONE.

Tyrant I do!

Poly
IT HAS MANY WINGS,
AND FRANKLY THINGS,
. . . ARE RUBBISH.

Everyone is silent and tense. Suddenly the **Tyrant** *applauds, her eyes filling with tears.*

Tyrant (*genuinely moved*) Oh!!! It's like you've put your hands around my soul. See, I'm not bad! I'm just misunderstood and my parents have never said well done, even when I conquered the southern legions of the Macedonian kingdom. And you, my dear friends! My behaviour has been appalling.

Can you ever forgive me?

Beat.

Atlas Of course.

Poly Are we free to go?

Tyrant On one condition! That we all work together.

Poly How?

Tyrant You have actors, a writer, a director but there's someone missing! I shall be your producer! I will send you across the world and you will play the biggest arenas and be paid riches beyond your wildest dreams, or at least riches in line with the minimums proscribed by your unions. You must tell this very tale, the one I have just witnessed! The story of a brother and sister, of loves lost and found and lost again, of wicked betrayal and glorious redemption and of a Tyrant who become a friend. Oh, Thespis there is a world of fame waiting for you out there! All you have to do is say yes. The choice is yours . . .

Beat. Musical spike.

Thespis I can't. For you see the choice isn't mine. I didn't come up with acting –

Atlas Technically I did.

Thespis We all did and so we must all decide together. What do you say everyone?

Poly I'm in.

Atlas I'm in.

Puts their hand in.

Adonis I'm in.

Tyrant I'm in.

Put their hands in.

Melampus The show must go on! That's it!! The show must go on!

Adonis Nailed it.

They high five.

FINALE

Melampus
WE'LL RENT OUT A BOAT!
PRACTISE OUR SCENES.

Poly
GO TOUR THE WORLD
FROM ROME TO MILTON KEYNES.

Atlas
AND THEY'LL SEE FOR THEMSELVES.
HOW WE NEARLY GOT BURNT.

Melampus
ALL OUR MISTAKES
ALL THE THINGS WE LEARNT.

Poly
WE'LL TOUR AS A TROUPE,

Thespis
LIVING THE DREAM.

Adonis
GO AS A GROUP
LEAVE AS A TEAM

Poly
SHOW THEM THE WORLD EXACTLY AS IT IS.

Thespis
WE'LL MAKE A SHOW,
THEY'LL WATCH THE SHOW.

Poly
THAT'S WHAT TOURING IS!

Music shifts. **Thespis** *sings to* **Atlas**.

Thespis
THERE'S A WORLD OUT THERE, ATLAS,
THERE'S A WORLD OUT THERE!

Atlas
SO YOU'VE SAID, THESPIS . . .

Thespis
A MAGIC WORLD,
SOMEWHERE OUT THERE.

Atlas
SOMEWHERE OUT THERE.

Thespis
AND HOW GLAD I'LL BE TO BE THERE,
MY HEART WILL BURST WITH PRIDE . . .

Atlas
AND SO WILL MINE.

Thespis
'CAUSE EVERYTHING I SEE THERE,
YOU'LL BE THERE BY MY SIDE.

Atlas
I'LL BE THERE.

Thespis
AND NO MATTER WHERE WE GO,
ONE THING WILL BE TRUE.

Atlas What?

Thespis
THAT MY WORLD IS YOU.

A musical build. They kiss. We go to **Adonis**, **Poly** *and* **Melampus**.

Poly
WHAT THINGS
WE HAVE SEEN
ON OUR JOURNEY . . .

Melampus
SO FAR . . .!

Poly
THAT LIFE CAN BE GREAT . . .

Melampus
IT'S NEVER TOO LATE . . .

Adonis
TO BE WHO WE ARE!

Atlas
TO BE WHO WE ARE!

Adonis
AND SWAPPING OUR SHOES
HAS SHOWN,
HOW BETTER TO
WEAR OUR OWN

Poly
THE PEOPLE WE WERE,

Melampus
ARE NOT WHO WE ARE,

Poly
WE'VE FOUND WHO WE ARE!

Melampus
WE'VE FOUND WHO WE ARE!

Adonis
WE'VE FOUND WHO WE ARE!

Lyrics begin to overlap.

Thespis
OPEN YOUR HEARTS,
OPEN YOUR MIND
NOTICE YOUR NEIGHBOUR,
WHAT DO YOU FIND?

Atlas
OPEN YOUR HEARTS,
OPEN YOUR MIND
NOTICE YOUR NEIGHBOUR,
WHAT DO YOU FIND?

Adonis
NOTICE YOUR NEIGHBOUR,
WHAT DO YOU FIND?

Bard *and* **Rhapsodes** *enter.*

Thespis, Atlas, Adonis, Bard
PEEL OFF THE PEEL,
THAT IS THE KEY,
FEEL WHAT THEY FEEL,
SEE WHAT THEY SEE.

Melampus, Poly, Tyrant, Rhapsodes
AHH

All

DON'T LIVE IN DOUBT,
TRY EVERY TURN.
THINGS DON'T WORK OUT,
WHAT DID YOU LEARN?

Poly

I LEARNT TO LEAD.

Thespis

I LEARNT MY LESSON!

Atlas

I LEARNT TO LIVE.

Melampus

I LEARNT TO LIVE RIGHT NOW!

Tyrant

I LEARNT TO CHILL

Atlas

I GREW A BACKBONE!

Melampus

LEARNT TO MOVE ON.

Adonis

LEARNT NOT TO DOUBLE DOWN.

Thespis

I LEARNT TO LOVE.

Poly

I LEARNT TO SEE.

Adonis

I LEARNT TO BE MYSELF.

Melampus

I LEARNT TO SEIZE THE DAY.

All

I ACT LIKE YOU!
YOU ACT LIKE ME!
THAT'S WHAT A MUSICAL IS!

Musical flourish.

Bard And so they toured the world!

Rhapsodes Previewing in Crete en route to Cairo.

Bard Stopping off in Hong Kong and Rio de Janeiro.

Rhapsodes Playing for a month or day.

Bard Hitting the West End and even Broadway!

Rhapsodes Culminating in tonight's performance at the Mercury Theatre Colchester!

All

WE ARE THE TRAVELLING THESPIANS!
TOURING A TOWN AT A TIME.

AND SHARING OUR STORY AMONG OUR PEERS,
TO NIGHTLY OVATIONS,
AND CRIES AND CHEERS,
ON A TOUR THAT LASTS SEVERAL THOUSAND YEARS!

AND NOW WE'RE HERE!
AND NOW WE'RE HERE!

THOSE TALENTED,
TRAVELLING THESPIANS,
FLOATING AROUND ON A DIME.

WE'VE TREATED YOU ALL TO SOME HEART AND HAM,
SO IF YOU ENJOYED IT BEFORE YOU SCRAM,
PLEASE POST YOUR PICTURES ON INSTAGRAM,
IT HELPS OUR SALES!
IT HELPS OUR SALES!

Kick line.

LET'S HEAR SOME LOVE FOR THE THESPIANS,
MAY WE NEVER HAVE REASON TO CEASE!

THE STAGIEST,
HAPPIEST,
CAMPIEST,
SCRAPPIEST,

FIRST EVER ACTORS
OF GREECE . . .
OF GREECE . . .
OF GREECE!

Bard
STANDING OVATION!

Rhapsodes What's that?

Bard This!

Blackout.

Lights up to standing ovation.

Bows.

End

www.ingramcontent.com/pod-product-compliance
Lightning Source LLC
LaVergne TN
LVHW052341100826
845147LV00021B/1142

* 9 7 8 1 3 5 0 6 5 2 4 0 8 *